JUSTICE SEEKERS, PEACE MAKERS

MICHAEL TRUE

justice
seekers
peace
makers

**32 PORTRAITS
IN COURAGE**

TWENTY-THIRD PUBLICATIONS
Mystic, Connecticut

ACKNOWLEDGMENTS

I am grateful to a number of people who helped with this book, especially my associates at Assumption College who provided support and assistance in writing. I am particularly grateful to Richard Oehling, Michael O'Shea, Roger Trahan, Pearl Phillips, and Jill Lepore, as well as to the editors of *Commonweal, America, Christian Century,* and *Worcester Magazine,* where several of these portraits appeared in different form. Mary Pat True helped, as always, in putting the manuscript into shape; she also bears some responsibility for the dedication.

Second printing November 1985

© 1985 by Michael True. All rights reserved. No part of this publication may be reproduced in any manner without prior written permission of the publisher. Write to Permissions Editor, P.O. Box 180, Mystic CT 06355.

Library of Congress Catalog Card Number 84-52708
ISBN 0-89622-212-8

Edited by Helen Coleman
Designed by John G. van Bemmel
Cover design by George Herrick

Photo credits: front cover—all the property of Assumption College, Worcester, Mass. except the handcuffing of Frances Crowe, © 1983 Nancy and Paul Clover; back cover—Assumption College, Worcester, Mass.; interior—p. 25, Winslow Martin; p. 55, Tom Foley; p. 82, Molly Culligan.

Acknowledgments: Poems by Daniel Berrigan reprinted by permission of the author. Poems by Stanley Kunitz reprinted from *Collected Poems* (The Atlantic Monthly Press) by permission of the author. "Poem" reprinted from *The Speed of Darkness* by Muriel Rukeyser by permission of International Creative Management, Inc. © 1968 by Muriel Rukeyser.

DEDICATION

This book is for

Mary
Michael
John
Christopher
Elizabeth
Anne

CONTENTS

INTRODUCTION

Every age collects its heroes and heroines, who serve as examples for tasks that need doing. In a violent age, we do well to remember those peacemakers and justice-seekers whom we might look to for inspiration and guidance. Internationally famous or relatively unknown, they worked for the common good. Because of them, others enjoy some semblance of hope, a possible future.

The backgrounds and talents of the thirty-two men and women in this collection of portraits, mostly Americans of the past 200 years, are diverse: pamphleteers, teachers, homemakers, poets, workers. The youngest died at twenty-four; the oldest lived into his late nineties. Several married; others had children born out of wedlock; a few were celibate. At times, they led lives as chaotic and faltering as our own. Their concerns, however, were and are the major issues of the day: slavery, racial and sexual discrimination, militarism, economic exploitation.

The point is not that they are flawless (although a couple of them were saints), but that in times of suffering or happiness, failure or success, they upheld values on the side of life. They spoke truth to power and exposed injustices associated with war and oppression. Even with their obvious limitations and inconsistencies, these women and men make it easier for us to be good.

Our problem at present, as Gordon Zahn has said, is not a lack of heroes and heroines, but our failure to recognize them when they appear in our midst. In addressing this neglect, this state of non-recognition, I call attention to several people always on the verge of disappearing—not because of death, but because of annihilation of memory. Even those famous in their own time are soon forgotten, and many apostles of nonviolent direct action, deservedly admired, are confined by history to local status, even when their contributions to social change were considerable.

1

A note on arrangement and choices: The book begins with John Leary, the last born (1958), and moves back to Thomas Paine, the earliest born (1737). The contemporary figures, especially, are rather selective, including some people I have known by accident of living in one area of the country. Others I have learned about in teaching literature, especially writers who combine a dedication to craft and to social justice. With these artists, life and writing are one; each gathers strength from the other, so that their readers are doubly blessed. Their work belongs to any humane culture in the making.

A principal reason for this book is "to save" the lives of thirty-two people, and to provide a reminder, I hope, of better values, of wiser men and women. Remembering them and their example helps one "image" a human future—one that is just and peaceful, the only one we should settle for. By their patience and persistence, they bring that better world into being. The work of sustaining it is the responsibility of the rest of us.

*   *   *

Note: The lists of books by and about the various figures at the end of each essay are selective. The words "And others" after primary sources mean simply that the person's writings go far beyond the concerns reflected in this particular listing. The arrangement of books by the subject is chronological, more recent publications first. The arrangement of books about the subject is alphabetical.

I have tried to mention items that are easily accessible, including standard biographies and bibliographies available in most larger libraries. Many of the people appear also in standard reference volumes, especially *Contemporary Authors* and *Current Biography;* historical figures are discussed in *Notable American Women, Dictionary of American Biography,* or *Dictionary of National Biography.*

JOHN LEARY

1958-1982

JOHN HENRY NEWMAN, VICTORIAN SAGE AND WRITER, ONCE SAID of extraordinary men and women that their thoughts, words, acts, trials, and fortunes have a charm to everyone, and "a power of exercising and eliciting the latent elements of Divine Grace" in others that nothing else can. The appeal of a young person who elicits such a response is even stronger. Among people who knew him during his short life, this was particularly true of John Timothy Leary, who died on August 31, 1982, at twenty-four years of age. Within a year of his death, a Catholic Worker House in Boston had been named for him, as well as the annual award of the New England Peace Fellowship, which he himself had received at the annual conference at Yale University in 1981.

During his years as an undergraduate at Harvard, John Leary had made himself indispensable to a number of peace and justice organizations in New England, often doing the jobs that students are asked to perform, driving "important people" to and from the airport, distributing leaflets and press releases prior to vigils and demonstrations, and begging for food for the various soup kitchens where he cooked and served poor and hungry street people. Father Daniel Berrigan's experience, described in an elegy for John Leary, is representative. At one of their meetings they talked at length "of resistance and faith and such realities. He also brought me to Haley House once to meet with a young sailor who had deserted a nuclear craft for reasons of conscience and needed a little lift of the heart and some evidence of friendship."

Gordon Zahn, whom John Leary worked closely with at the Pax Christi Center on Conscience and War in Cambridge, Massachusetts, called him "a different kind of hero."

> In a very real sense what we refer to as "the Movement" would not move much at all were it not for those who, like John, are always there to set up the literature tables, re-arrange the chairs, run the duplicator, deliver the slides and projector, pick up the leaflets, and then spend hours on some street corner distributing them to usually unrecep-tive passersby.

Born in Vernon, Connecticut, February 22, 1958, the youngest child of an Irish-Catholic working-class family, John Leary became involved in local political issues by the seventh grade. He wrote for the Rockville High School newspaper, ran with the track team, and joined the debating society, and was voted "most respected" by the senior class of 1976. Somewhat surprised to find himself at Harvard University, he nonetheless did well there, eventually graduating with honors and completing a senior thesis on the nonviolent tradition in Christianity. His commitment to social justice began with his work as a volunteer in a tutoring project for prisoners, conducted by Phillips Brooks House at Harvard. From there he turned to other "life" issues, including resistance to nuclear weapons and to abortion.

The rooms and apartments John shared, sometimes with students, sometimes with other residents of Boston and Cambridge, were open to street people, with as many as twenty men and women sleeping on the floor during the winter. The Reverend John Marsh described one occasion when "lice had found the apartment a good place to transfer from one human body to another, and one of the neighbors had tried to burn the building down in order to prevent 'those fumes from coming around here.'" When that particular experiment ended, Leary devoted more time to the Pax Christi Center, where he counselled young men his age facing the draft and visited schools to speak on issues related to conscription. At the same time, he worked in the soup kitchen at Haley House, a Catholic Worker House in Boston; attended a weekly vigil, occasionally risking arrest for civil disobedience at Draper Laboratories; served on planning committees for various organizations, including the New England Catholic Peace Fellowship; and attended religious retreats, Sunday liturgies at a Melkite congregation, and daily mass at local Catholic parishes around Boston. At graduation from college, he received the Ames Award, given to a senior recognized by Harvard University for public service.

These activities indicate the variety and seriousness of John Leary's commitment to social justice and the extent of his personal associations as a young man. But they do not convey the manner and tone of his personality or the depth of his commitment to nonviolent love. Nor do they suggest the kind of admiration he evoked from his associates or the humor, youth, vulnerability, and strength that characterized his dealings with people of all ages. A spirit of reconciliation, of sweet reasonableness, flowed over into all his activities. During an anti-draft sit-in at a South Boston post office, for example, when he was beaten by several men his own age, he characteristically refused to bring charges against them.

At such times, John said, he was consoled by the repetition of a prayer he had come across in his studies: "Lord Jesus Christ, Son of the Living God, have mercy on me a sinner."

The incongruity of John Leary's judging himself harshly, while leading a life that everyone recognized as exemplary, was part of his charm.

Retaining a clear sense of the world and an appreciation for its better moments, he still kept a bit of distance on it, with a clear critique of its willful and casual cruelties and a vivid understanding of the healing that must take place if it is ever to improve.

Such diversity of spirit, youthful yet mature, caught the attention of his associates, several of whom have written about him since he died, unexplainably, while jogging in Cambridge in late summer, 1982.

Father Daniel Berrigan, echoing the noble lines of "Lycidas," Milton's elegy for a promising fellow student, wrote of John Leary, in a "Journey to Block Island":

> Rare spirit, rare
> Harvard College had not his peer
> "An award for drowning do-gooders,"
> when honors came his way . . .
> wits end, at such ending
> of promise, sweetness, surmise
> fantasy take hold—
> John Leary at cliff side
> life's headlong venture
> by no means stilled.

John Leary is remembered as one of the many young people who revitalized the peace movement in the 1980s. Because he died young, perhaps, his example seems especially poignant, just as a skilled artist's work appears more mysterious (one thinks of Keats, Wilfred Owen) in a brief life. More dramatically, if purposefully, it reveals what any life informed by noble values might be—for a single moment or for a long period of time.

By John Leary

"How Can Church Support Draft Non-registrants?" *National Catholic Reporter,* August 13, 1982.

About John Leary

Cheryl R. Devall, "The Gospel According to John," *Harvard Crimson* 1981 Commencement Issue, p. 37.

John Leary: A Different Sort of Hero. Cambridge, Mass.: Pax Christi USA Center on Conscience and War, 1983, and Erie, Pa.: Net Press, 1983.

ELIZABETH MCALISTER
1939-

AND

PHILIP BERRIGAN
1923-

REARING A FAMILY AND LIVING A LIFE OF RESISTANCE TO militarism are usually regarded as mutually exclusive vocations. And certainly challenging the status quo in the larger culture while trying to maintain that most traditional social unit, the family, calls for special sacrifice and planning.

Certainly marriages between people with more traditional

careers suffer conflicts that undermine the cooperative spirit essential to marriage and to bringing up children. Persistent questions about where the family will live, who will diaper which child, and which bills should be paid when present themselves with even greater urgency when one parent is on trial for civil disobedience, for example, and another is preparing to serve a sentence in federal prison for acts of resistance at a nuclear weapons plant.

In an age requiring citizen action to prevent the annihilation of humankind, parents have begun to face complex questions about how to live lives of resistance. In the United States, no one knows the risks of such choices better than Elizabeth McAlister and Philip Berrigan, parents of three children, whose decision to marry was made in the shadow of resistance.

Even their courtship took place under the surveillance of the Federal Bureau of Investigation, in 1970, while Philip was in Allenwood (Pennsylvania) Federal Prison for the destruction of draft files, and while Elizabeth faced charges of conspiring to blow up tunnels under the U.S. Capitol Building in Washington D.C. He was eventually released from jail, and she was cleared of all charges in the Harrisburg 8 trial, but not before their love letters were published to the world at a time when Philip Berrigan was still arguing the advantages of celibacy for non-violent resisters.

In May and June 1969, Philip Berrigan said in an interview that celibacy was ''crucial in the priesthood as an aid for revolutionary lifestyle,'' and complained about married men who turned down opportunities for acts of resistance. ''And almost invariably the question of family obligations comes up, children, etc. So we feel celibacy can be a great freedom in a public forum.''

For skeptics, such conflicts between public statements and private behavior merely confirmed their suspicions about the priest-turned-revolutionary. Among Catholics, the fact that Elizabeth McAlister was a nun at the time of their marriage brought additional public criticism. Could any union survive such religious and political turmoil? The obvious answer is that for well over a decade, theirs has, through the birth of three children, numerous arrests, trials, and imprisonments, not to mention the traditional tests "in sickness and in health" or, in the words of the famous hymn, "through dungeon, fire, and sword."

"When we accepted each other," Philip Berrigan wrote after their marriage, "that included acceptance of our work in resistance and its consequences: discipline, risk, separation, jail." For both of them, war resistance is a continuation of a religious vocation that has been central to their lives for many years.

Philip Berrigan, born in Two Harbors, Minnesota, on October 5, 1923, is the youngest of six brothers, having grown up, like his brother Daniel, in Syracuse, New York. After parochial schools in Syracuse, Philip attended the University of Toronto for a year, and then enlisted in the U.S. Army during World War II. A paratrooper in Europe, he witnessed the destruction of Dresden by allied bombers, an event that made a deep impression on him.

In 1947, Philip Berrigan returned to undergraduate studies; following graduation from the College of the Holy Cross in 1950, he entered the Society of St. Joseph, a religious order with a particular ministry to black people. He taught high school in New Orleans, where he served also as a parish priest, and eventually became involved in the Civil Rights movement through the Congress of Racial Equality and the Southern Christian Leadership Conference and, later, the Community for Nonviolent Action and the Fellowship of Reconciliation. Prevented by his religious superiors from participating in the march in Selma, Alabama, in 1965, he was subsequently brought "home" to the North, taught at the Josephite seminary, amid controversy, in Newburgh, New York, and then was assigned to an all-black parish in Baltimore, Maryland. There, encouraging self-determination among the neighborhood's black community, he became deeply involved in justice issues once again.

Among Berrigan's co-workers were Tom Lewis, an artist, and two others who joined them in the first nonviolent destruction of draft files, in Baltimore, in the fall of 1967. While under indictment, Berrigan and Lewis joined seven others in burning draft files in nearby Catonsville, Maryland, on May 17, 1968. This event, famous in the movement against the war in Vietnam, led to a long trial and imprisonment. Berrigan was shipped from place to place and was spied on by fellow prisoners; one of them handed over love letters and other documents to the F.B.I. during the time Philip and Elizabeth were making plans to marry.

Elizabeth McAlister, at the time of their marriage, had been a member of the Religious of the Sacred Heart of Mary for thirteen years. She joined the order after graduating from Lacordaire Academy, Montclair, New Jersey, and attending Marymount College, Tarrytown, New York, both of which were owned by the religious order.

Born on November 17, 1939, in Orange, New Jersey, one of seven children, Elizabeth McAlister was chosen early in her career for special responsibilities in the religious order. After finishing an M.A. degree at Hunter College, she taught art history for seven years at her alma mater, and then served as provincial secretary for the order. Her duties included working on various assignments associated with church renewal and the Second Vatican Council. In the meantime, she became involved also in resistance to the Vietnam war, speaking, leafletting, demonstrating, and marching for peace.

Married on April 7, 1969 in St. George's Episcopal Church in the Bronx, Elizabeth McAlister and Philip Berrigan made no public announcement of the event until May 28, 1973. Shortly afterward, in Baltimore, where they have lived ever since, they founded Jonah House, a community committed to non-violent resistance against the arms race.

For over a decade, Jonah House has been a center for education and an example for the resistance movement, a kind of "think tank" and an inspiration for the wider community. There, in a two-story row house, the couple and their three children have harbored a succession of people who have been in and out of jail for civil disobedience. Throughout, they have maintained an almost continuous peace witness at the Pentagon, at the Presidential "Blight House," and at various war industries along the Atlantic seaboard. Since 1980, Philip and Elizabeth have joined Plowshares groups who have taken nonviolent resistance another step by damaging weapons at various military industries and bases in the Northeast.

Their continuing publication, *Year One,* a modest,

mimeographed compendium of poems, essays, religious medita-
tions, and information, has been important to the movement
as well. Like previous publications in American history, Isaiah
Thomas's *Massachusetts Spy* during the Revolution, William Lloyd
Garrison's *The Liberator* and Abigail Kelley Foster's Anti-Slavery
Bugle during abolitionism, and Eugene Victor Debs's *An Appeal
to Reason,* in the labor movement, *Year One* tells the stories of
those resisting the injustices of the present. In the 19th century,
it was black slavery and wage slavery that provoked protests and
civil disobedience; in this century, it is war-making and the
"psychic numbing" that tolerates nuclearism.

All this activity, with people coming and going to speaking engagements, trials, and jail, continues alongside the family
and communal life of Jonah House. Although a tenth anniver-
sary announcement lamented the fact that "the harvest is ripe
but the laborers are few," the community can point to several
achievements in their persistent campaign and to the many lives
it has influenced. Throughout, Elizabeth McAlister and Philip
Berrigan have kept family life and contemplation central to their
vocations. They have not stopped the bomb, as they would be
the first to complain. But in the struggle for peace, they have
helped to secure a future for their children and for others.

Along the way, in their writings, they have been clear
about the power that sustains them. Just prior to her trial in
Syracuse, New York, in May 1984, for civil disobedience at Grif-
fiss Air Force Base the previous Thanksgiving, Elizabeth
McAlister wrote, for example:

> It becomes clearer and clearer that our hope summons us
> to specific works, to making history, when there is no longer
> any history possible. Hope is the primal mode of existence,
> not added to, but as necessary to life as breath itself for
> Christians. Hope means belief in the God of life.

By Elizabeth McAlister
and Philip Berrigan

Berrigan, Philip. *Widen the Prison Gates: Writing from Jails*, *April 1970 - December 1972*. New York: Simon and Schuster, 1973.

Berrigan, Philip. *A Punishment for Peace*. New York: Macmillan, 1969.

McAlister, Elizabeth. "Bringing Forth in Hope," *Year One*, X, No. 1 (January 1984), 4-7.

And others, including essays in their newsletter *Year One*, 1933 Park Avenue, Baltimore, Maryland 21217, 1973 - present.

About Elizabeth McAlister
and Philip Berrigan

du Plessix Gray, Francine. *Divine Disobedience*. New York: Random House, 1969.

Klejment, Anne. *The Berrigans: A Bibliography of Published Works by Daniel, Philip, and Elizabeth McAlister Berrigan*. New York: Garland Publishing Company, 1979.

Raines, John C., ed. *Conspiracy: The Implications of the Harrisburg Trial for the Democratic Tradition*. New York: Harper and Row, 1974.

Kathy Knight

1938-

THE INFLUENCES THAT BRING PEOPLE TO WORK FOR NONVIOLENT social changes are not always obvious even to the people themselves. Years later, thinking back on what started them on a long pilgrimage for social justice, however, they may point to one incident, person, or book that altered the direction of their lives. Kathy Knight, for example, a person who has been at the center of the Catholic peace movement in the Boston area for twenty years, remembers a day in 1965 that prompted her to study the history of America's involvement in Southeast Asia and eventually to alter the direction of her life.

One morning that summer, the face of a dear friend looked out at her from the pages of the *Boston Globe.* An American prisoner of war in Vietnam, he had been executed by the National Liberation Front in reprisal for the execution of a hero of the N.L.F. "Suddenly the war became real to me. I began reading to find out how it started and what it was all about, a process that led eventually to a change in career."

The discrepancies between the history of U.S. involvement in Vietnam and the slogans being used to justify the war shocked her. "In addition, I felt the scandal of the Catholic Church's apparent support of the war to be a kind of fundamental sin against the Holy Spirit," Knight said. "Sometimes it seemed like a crucifixion re-enacted."

From then on, the path that led to a career in peace education "was almost always clear, well-marked, and obvious," Knight added.

> I would have had to actively look for false trails to avoid it. The opportunities were there and so was my ability to use them. I never questioned that the strongest possible public witness against the massive evil of the Indochina war (and now nuclear arms race) was the required expression of my faith.

Born in the Philippines on December 29, 1938, and evacuated from Hong Kong in 1941, Kathy Kohlhas Knight grew up as "a navy brat," and graduated from high school in Norfolk, Virginia, where her father, a career navy man, was stationed. It was in Norfolk that she became friends with the young man, a devout Catholic and later West Point graduate, who was killed in Vietnam. She is well aware of the ironic circumstance that her work as a peacemaker was prompted by a friendship with a professional soldier, "the most virtuous young man I ever met."

In 1955, she went to college at Bryn Mawr, where she

completed both a B.A. and an M.A. in English, and where she met her husband, Charles Knight, a student at Haverford College and a conscientious objector to military service. Both were converts to Catholicism, with expectations of careers as literary scholars. After teaching at the University of Massachusetts, Amherst, they moved to Newton, Massachusetts, in 1965, where they have lived ever since. "I look back on the irony of the fact that it was because I was then at home, with four small children, rather than under a teaching contract, that I was 'free' to become intensely active in the anti-war movement."

Later, after six years with the American Friends Service Committee, a Quaker organization, Kathy Knight chose to work on justice and peace issues in a less favorable, more needy environment, that is, the Catholic community: (1) arranging for speakers and films on draft counseling and the history of the Vietnam War, and conducting workshops on Catholic social teaching related to these issues; (2) lobbying locally and in Washington for specific legislation to reduce the military budget and to build a peace economy; (3) participating in direct action through vigils, demonstrations, and civil disobedience to stop American intervention in Cambodia and Laos, and later in Central America. "Since Vatican II, the church has developed a strong official teaching about the centrality of justice and peace to the Christian mission, but the teaching remained unknown to most of the faithful."

Initially a volunteer for the local and regional Catholic Peace Fellowships, then on the staff of the official Boston archdiocesan commission, she now helps to direct the Catholic Connection, a reflection/action center for justice and peace in a Boston suburb. All of this is maintained, of course, while helping to bring four children through the teenage and into their college years.

Although she gave up a career as a teacher of English twenty years ago, Kathy Knight regards her present work as an extension of that earlier vocation. Her approach to social justice is not a prophetic one, in other words, but simply "an attempt to get the facts straight." Such work involves understanding the foreign and military policies that have accompanied the expansion of American power since World War II, including the more recent agony in El Salvador, "the latest example in a very long list. I believe that the injustice and human suffering caused by this trend would justify the lifelong careers of legions of citizens like myself. The same logic applies to the nuclear arms issue, where the stakes of the struggle are incredibly higher."

People she has known along the path toward a "social change profession," especially priests and religious who put their lives on the line, have dramatized for Knight the close link between social and religious issues. Anthony Mullaney, James Harney, and Robert Cunnane, for example, who were arrested for burning draft files in Milwaukee in 1968, provided alternatives "to the horrendous institution that was getting it all wrong." In the late 1970's other individuals and signs made it easy to put things in perspective. Being a close friend of Maura Clark, one of the four women killed in El Salvador in 1982, and knowing John Leary, a young Catholic Worker in Boston, provided the moral encouragement, she said, that others often gain from spiritual reading and prayer.

Working closely with people of faith enriched and confirmed Knight's life. No matter how much virtue or courage her most militant associates exhibited, she found that they all possessed areas of great fallibility. She could view them as heroic or even as saints, but not necessarily feel obliged to adopt their approaches to peacemaking.

She has not, for example, confronted sexism as directly as other women, she thinks, partly because she never questioned her ability to pursue a career of her own choice. She went to a good college, one where the suffragette movement and movements for social change were regarded as appropriate and even admirable.

At forty-six, she speaks also with considerable assurance about her religious faith. "I am a person who has never really undergone a crisis of faith. From the time I was about six, I recognized that I needed the security that faith in God provided. I don't look on that state of affairs as invalidating my faith, but in it I simply acknowledge that the Holy Spirit works with the negatives as well as the positives of human personality and experience." In this, as in the ironic beginnings of her career as a peacemaker, Kathy Knight is attuned to the diversity of human experience and the many paths by which people arrive at their vocation.

BY KATHY KNIGHT

"Speaking Truth to Power," *Bryn Mawr Alumni Bulletin,* Spring, 1982, 8-10.

MARTIN LUTHER KING, JR.

1929-1968

MAKING MARTIN LUTHER KING, JR.'S BIRTHDAY A NATIONAL holiday recognized the importance of his life and writings. Thinking back on his relatively brief public life, one is sometimes astonished to remember that the Civil Rights movement was already fifteen years old when he became its central figure. Still a young man in 1956, he emerged as the principal spokesperson of a host of equally remarkable men and women.

Yet by background and training, Martin Luther King, Jr. was especially well prepared to make the most of that nonviolent revolution which, in transforming the South, provided a training ground, a school, a university-without-walls for social change. Just as the Wobblies, socialists, and anarchists in the decade before the First World War educated labor organizers and reformers for the radical 30s, so the new abolitionists of the Civil Rights movement taught a later generation about nonviolent resistance and agitation for change.

Looking over the names of leaders in the antiwar and draft resistance movements, as well as in later campaigns against the nuclear arms race, one can point to many who went South during the 1960s, on Freedom Rides, in voter registration campaigns or the March on Selma. Philip Berrigan, for example, taught in a black school in New Orleans before he burned draft files in Maryland; Abby Hoffman ran a "Snick" (Student Nonviolent Coordinating Committee) shop, selling crafts from Mississippi before he initiated his "revolution for the hell of it" on the Lower East Side in Manhattan; Howard Zinn and Staughton Lynd taught in a black women's college in Atlanta before Zinn joined Resist in Boston and Lynd became a labor lawyer in Youngstown, Ohio. Similarly, Rosa Parks disobeyed an Alabama law against blacks and Fannie Lou Hamer challenged traditional roles of women in Mississippi before Betty Friedan and Gloria Steinem wrote a line.

"The son, the grandson, and the great-grandson of preachers," as he so tactfully reminded the clergymen addressed in "Letter from Birmingham Jail," Martin Luther King, Jr., was born on January 15, 1929, in Atlanta, Georgia. Educated at Morehouse College there and Crozer Theological Seminary in Pennsylvania, he was ordained a Baptist minister in his father's church at 18. In 1955, he completed a doctorate in systematic theology at Boston University. That December, he called a citywide boycott of segregated buses in Montgomery, Alabama, where he had been serving as pastor of a church for over a year. From then until his death in Memphis in 1968, he coordinated and inspired nonviolent movement for social change focusing on the rights of working people, especially blacks, and resistance to the American war in Southeast Asia.

King's power is evident, not only in his extraordinary courage, but also in his skills as a speaker and writer. His essays, for example, lose little of their effect even years after the events that prompted them have been forgotten. "The Negro Revolution," (1963), characteristic in style and language, makes its point through stories from his own life and those of his associates: "Some years ago," King begins,

> I sat in a Harlem department store, surrounded by hundeds of people. I was autographing copies of *Stride Toward Freedom,* my book about the Montgomery bus boycott of 1955-56. As I signed my name to a page, I felt something sharp plunge forcefully into my chest. I had been stabbed with a letter opener, struck home by a woman who would later be judged insane. Rushed by ambulance to Harlem Hospital, I lay in a bed for hours while preparations were made to remove the keen-edged knife from my body. Days later, when I was well enough to talk with Dr. Aubrey Maynard, the chief of surgeons who performed the delicate, dangerous operation, I learned the reason for the long delay that preceded surgery. He told me that the razor tip of the instrument had been touching my aorta and that my whole chest had to be opened to extract it. "If you had sneezed during all those hours of waiting," Maynard said, "your aorta would have been punctured and you would have drowned in your own blood." In the summer of 1963, the knife of violence was just that close to the nation's aorta.

Although King's name and achievement are known to many people, the deeper implications of his life, as with those of many peacemakers, are often trivialized or forgotten. This is particularly true of his deep, persistent commitment to non-violence. Fortunately, however, in *Stride Toward Freedom* (1958), he gives an account of his spiritual odyssey, beginning with his reading of Thoreau in college, and moving on to his reading of Marx, Gandhi, and Reinbold Niebuhr, and hearing A.J. Muste in the seminary.

Although he sided with Gandhi, he had to come to terms

with Niebuhr's critique of pacifism. In the intellectual struggle that ensued, King noticed that Niebuhr ''interpreted pacifism as a sort of passive resistance to evil expressing naive trust in the power of love. But this was a serious distortion,'' King concluded.

> My study of Gandhi convinced me that true pacifism is not non-resistance to evil, but nonviolent resistance to evil. Between the two positions, there is a world of difference. Gandhi resisted evil with as much vigor and power as the violent resister, but he resisted with love instead of hate. True pacifism is not unrealistic submission to evil power, as Niebuhr contends. It is rather a courageous confrontation of evil by the power of love. . . .

Just how fully King took this principle to heart is indicated not only by his rejection of violence in the struggle for black equality, but also in his resistance to the war in Vietnam. The piece of writing for which he is best remembered, however, is a classic essay, equal in power and eloquence to the Declaration of Independence and Thoreau's ''Civil Disobedience.'' ''Letter from Birmingham Jail'' (1963), addressed to eight Protestant, Catholic, and Jewish clergymen who called King's leadership ''unwise and untimely,'' describes the historical, religious, and political justifications for his actions and helped thereby to win a nation to his cause. Reprinted in newsletters, newspapers, pamphlets, and books, it became the *Common Sense* of the second American revolution.

In bringing together the principles of 19th century American abolitionists and nonresisters—Garrison, Thoreau, Ballou—and the practical teachings of Tolstoy and Gandhi, King gave the tradition of nonviolence a new and solid grounding in the American experience. In any nonviolent campaign, he says near the beginning of ''Letter from Birmingham Jail,'' there are four basic steps: ''(1) collection of the facts to determine whether injustices are alive; (2) negotiation; (3) self-purification; and (4) direct action.'' Then King shows how he and his associates met each of those conditions in Birmingham, and concludes with this argument for the justice of the black liberation movement:

Before the pilgrims landed at Plymouth, we were here. Before the pen of Jefferson etched the majestic words of the Declaration of Independence across the pages of history, we were here. For more than two centuries our forebearers labored in this country without wages; they made cotton king; they built the homes of their masters while suffering gross injustice and shameful humiliation— yet out of a bottomless vitality they continued to thrive and develop. If the inexpressible cruelties of slavery could not stop us, the opposition we now face will surely fail. We will win our freedom because the sacred heritage of our nation and the eternal will of God are embodied in our echoing demands.

BY MARTIN LUTHER KING, JR.

Speeches by the Rev. Dr. Martin Luther King, Jr., About the War in Vietnam. Arrendale: The Turnpike Press, n.d.

Where Do We Go From Here: Chaos or Community. New York: Harper and Row, 1967.

Why We Can't Wait. New York: Harper and Row, 1963 and New York: Signet books, 1964. See especially "Letter from Birmingham Jail."

Stride Toward Freedom: The Montgomery Story. New York: Harper and Row, 1958.

And others.

ABOUT MARTIN LUTHER KING, JR.

David L. Lewis, *King: A Critical Biography.* New York: Praeger, 1970.

Stephen B. Oates. *Let the Trumpet Sound: The Life of Martin Luther King, Jr.* New York: Harper and Row, 1982.

Martin Luther King, Jr.: A Documentary: Montgomery to Memphis. Edited by Flip Schulke. New York: W.W. Norton Co., 1976.

HOWARD ZINN

1922-

IN HOWARD ZINN, THE AGE OF DEMOCRACY HAS ITS AMERICAN
historian, a writer and teacher attuned to the forces that just
might create a world with respect for equality and human rights.
Unlike many historians, he fixes attention not on wars and
government, but on the ideas, imagination, and courage of ordinary people. And in a host of articles, essays, and books

published since 1959, he focuses on acts of disobedience and solidarity of the past two centuries that initiated mass movements for liberation. Confronted with such large popular movements against injustice, the established order—and sometimes even the state—has given way to reason and reform.

In charting this history, Howard Zinn commits something more than his voice and tenure as an academic, beginning with his active involvement in the civil rights movement and moving on to resistance against the draft and the nuclear arms race. With a handful of talented and committed academics and artists, including Noam Chomsky, Grace Paley, Denise Levertov, George Wald, and Richard Falk, Zinn makes the link between scholarship and humane values, between the academy and the public order. He is, in fact, almost a National Endowment for the Humanities himself.

Born in New York City on August 24, 1922, Zinn has lived in the Boston area, with his wife and family, since 1964. He, like many men of his generation, ''grew up'' in the armed services, and was decorated as an air force bombardier in Central Europe during the Second World War. Afterward, he completed his formal education at New York University and Columbia University under the G.I. bill, receiving a Ph.D. in history in 1958. Before moving to Boston University, he chaired the history and social science department at Spelman College, in Atlanta; during those years, he was also deeply involved in the civil rights movement and wrote an important study of the Student Nonviolent Coordinating Committee, *SNCC: The New Abolitionists* (1964).

Prior to the publication of his major work, *A People's History of the United States* (1980), Zinn wrote frequently on politics and the social thought of the Great Depression and on the tradition of civil disobedience in American history. In February 1968, he, with Father Daniel Berrigan, arranged the release of three American prisoners of war in North Vietnam, during a special visit to that country. Since that time, Howard Zinn has testified on behalf of people on trial for resisting the draft or for damaging nuclear weapons equipment; and he has appeared in several films, such as *Holy Outlaw* (1970) and *Lovejoy's Nuclear War* (1976), that dramatize those issues. He is the author, as well, of a successful biographical drama about the anarchist, feminist, and pamphleteer, Emma Goldman.

In writing history, Zinn has taken his lead not from the announced purposes of governments, but from their actions, their deeds. He has been careful, for example, to note "the warring elements" of the American creed. By this he means a conflict between the *rhetorical* creed, represented by the Declaration of Independence ("all Men are created equal," the right to revolution, and so on) and the *working* creed. The hard evidence is

> that all men are created equal, except foreigners with whom we are at war, blacks who have not been signaled out for special attention, Indians who will not submit, inmates of prisons, members of the armed forces, and anyone without money.

In his writings, as well as in his undergraduate classes and public lectures, Zinn spells out the consequences of this dichotomy, especially America's failure to alter its allocation of power and wealth. He occasionally admits that changes take place within the narrow boundaries of profit-motivated capitalism, a paternalistic political system, an aggressive foreign policy, and "a social system based on a culture of prejudices concerning race, national origin, sex, age, and wealth."

Zinn's truths are obvious to many observers outside the United States, but few people profess them from "inside the whale," and even fewer from the hallowed groves of academe. Although his view of history is sometimes regarded as unorthodox, his authority as a teacher and writer has won him a wide audience among students and scholars, as well as a significant, perhaps permanent, place among modern historians. With E.P. Thomaspon, in England, Zinn has made the history of the working class visible in a way that it has seldom been since the 1930s.

In his histories, Zinn has always been explicit about his purpose and goal. In the introduction to *Postwar America: 1945-1971,* for example, after encouraging the reader to take an active part in making history, he poses two central questions:

> First, why did the United States, exactly as it became the

most heavily armed and wealthiest society in the world, run into so much trouble with its own people? From the late fifties to the early seventies, the nation experienced unprecedented black rebellion, student demonstrations, antiwar agitation, civil disobedience, prison uprising, and a widespread feeling that American civilization was faltering, or even in decay. And second, what are the possibilities, the visions, the beginnings of fresh directions for this country?

A decade later, Zinn continues to explore the implications of these radical questions. In the same quiet, measured voice, with an understated, even wry humor, he lectures to large classes of undergraduates, speaks at a rally against conscription on the Boston Common, or addresses an annual meeting of professional historians and political scientists. Patient and persistent, he appears confident that his message will get through, amid the conventional noise and chatter. In the long effort to get the facts straight and to keep alive the history of ordinary people, he behaves as if time were on his side, "as long," he might add, "as the bomb doesn't fall."

By Howard Zinn

A People's History of the United States. New York: Harper and Row, 1980.

Postwar America: 1945-1971. Indianapolis, Ind.: Bobbs-Merrill, 1973.

The Politics of History. Boston: The Beacon Press, 1970.

Disobedience and Democracy. New York: Random House, 1968.

"Three Prisoners: The Petty Route Home," *Nation,* CCVI, No. 14 (April 1968), 431-37.

SNCC: The New Abolitionists. Boston: The Beacon Press, 1964.

And others.

DANIEL BERRIGAN

1921-

IN AN ELEGY FOR HIS FATHER, WRITTEN IN DANBURY FEDERAL
Prison during Holy Week, 1971, Daniel Berrigan also sketched
his own portrait, an outline of a complex and talented person
under the influence of a somewhat distant parent. The poem
describes his father's fierce shortcomings, as well as his rich legacy
to six sons:

He exacted performance, promptitude,
deference to his moods
the family escutcheon stained with no shit.
The game was skillful (we never saw it so well
    played
elsewhere), he was commonly considered
the epitome of a just man.
We sat on our perches blinking like six marmosets.
There were scenes worthy of Conrad;
the decks shuddering;
the world coming to an end. . . .

The expression on the face of the marmoset, a wide-eyed, un-blinking creature, astonished by what's coming next, is recognizable as Daniel Berrigan's own. One has seen it in numerous photographs of him: at a demonstration, during a trial, from a pulpit, and at his arrest at Block Island after the months underground in 1970. It is a face that says, "Well, what do you know? Look what I've gotten myself in for this time: The Lord be praised."

An early poem conveys that sense of wonder and the singular manner that characterizes Father Berrigan. "Each day writes/ in my heart's core/ ineradicably, what it is to be man":

I tread my earth amazed: what land,
what skies are these, whose shifting weathers
now shrink my harvest to a stack of bones;
now weigh my life with glory?

Christ. . . your presence give
light to my eyeless mind, reason to my heart's
    rhyme.

For all his public activities, as poet, teacher, theologian, war resister, liturgist, Daniel Berrigan is a surprisingly private person. Since his eighteenth year, his vocation as Jesuit and priest has been the center of his life.

Born in Virginia, Minnesota, on May 9, 1921, to an Irish railroad man with a flair for poetry and drama, and a devout but willful German woman, Daniel Berrigan attended parochial schools in Syracuse, New York, after his family moved to a farm near there in the 1920s. His entry into the Jesuits in 1939 preceded the later religious vocations of his older brother Jerome and his younger brother Philip after the Second World War. The confined, quasi-militarist regime of the Jesuits surprised Daniel, but he did well as a student and began publishing poems in national periodicals while still in college.

Soon after his ordination as a priest in 1942, he taught French and English in Jesuit high schools in New Jersey and in Brooklyn, before joining the theology department at Lemoyne College, East Syracuse, in 1957. On a sabbatical leave in 1964, he served as a parish priest in France, where he had studied previously; he admired the worker priest movement. In further travel at this time behind the Iron Curtain, he found the church persecuted, but clear about its religious mission. Back in the United States, where his brother Philip had become involved in the Civil Rights movement, Daniel co-founded several national organizations opposed to the war in Vietnam. Disciplined by the church hierarchy in New York for these and other activities, he was exiled to South America, which only deepened his resistance to United States policies toward the Third World.

Returning home after six weeks, he became a controversial figure again by his acts of revolutionary nonviolence and through his influence on young people, former students and admirers who eventually followed him into jail for burning draft records. In the 1970s and 80s, Father Berrigan participated in numerous symbolic actions against the state, including the damaging of nuclear weapons systems, the subject of a film, *In the King of Prussia* (1982). He and his brother Philip have also been an inspiration for activists resisting the deployment of American nuclear missiles in Western Europe.

As a writer, Daniel Berrigan occupies a peculiar place in American letters. In spite of his honors, including the Lamont Poetry Prize in 1957, awarded to an outstanding first book by the Academy of American Poets, as well as the Meltzer, St. Thomas More, and Obie awards, he is seldom treated seriously as an artist by influential critics. Writing outside the prevailing manner (whichever one is dominant at the moment), he charts his own course as a poet. "Writing was as integral to his life in prison as counseling or rapping, or organizing, or listening to the anguish of a prison brother," Philip Berrigan wrote in the introduction to Daniel's *Prison Poems.*

Some readers regard Berrigan's perpetual testing of the boundaries of experience, his effrontery to good behavior, as mere personal orneriness. And, to be sure, there is a bit of the Modernist spirit, the impulse "to shake up the bourgeoise," about his style.

Yet it is this quality of expecting the unexpected and his refusal to accept traditional boundaries that accounts in part for Daniel Berrigan's hold on people's attention. Faced, like Herman Melville's Bartleby with the inevitable (in Berrigan's case, obeying the law, paying war taxes, and tolerating America's policy of Mutually Assured Destruction—MAD), he "prefers not to."

As an artist and activist, Daniel Berrigan seems to promise, in typical American fashion, the unexpected, the impossible. Who else would leave a job at Cornell University (in 1968), fly to Hanoi to rescue three American flyers, return to a small suburb of Baltimore to burn draft records with homemade napalm, go through a long trial, and then, in costume to evade the FBI, slip underground? Narrowly escaping accidental death in prison, he embarked soon afterward on another series of non-violent actions, smashing missile warheads and risking jail numerous times while out on appeal. This is attended, along the way, by an outpouring of poems, essays, letters to periodicals, an award-winning play, several films, numerous lectures, and religious retreats, a variety of jobs (an orderly in a cancer hospital, and teaching assignments at leading universities) and close associations with a multitude of friends, family, and fellow resisters in this country and Europe.

If, as Wordsworth said, "the child is father of the man," some insight into Daniel Berrigan is provided by the self-portrait mentioned earlier. Equally significant is the famous statement of the Catonsville Nine, beginning, "The violence stops here, and death stops here, this war stops here."

We shall beyond doubt be placed behind bars for some

portion of our natural lives in consequence of our inability to live and die content in the plagued city, to say ''peace, peace'' when there is no peace, to keep the poor poor, the thirsty and hungry thirsty and hungry. Our apologies good friends for the fracture of good order, the burning of paper instead of children, the angering of the orderlies in the front parlor of the charnel house. We could not, so help us God, do otherwise.

The last statement—that he ''could not do otherwise''—suggests that, unlike other figures in the history of American radicalism from Thomas Paine to Dorothy Day, who chose their fates, Berrigan regards his as a given. Is this the reason for his rather ''Zen'' attitude toward it all?

In a nuclear age, Daniel Berrigan charts a new errand into the wilderness, a journey to Catonsville, attempting to turn ''lights on in the house of the dead.'' Even now, in his mid-60s, he is a figure to watch with expectation. Where will his fate carry him next?

BY DANIEL BERRIGAN

Lights on in the House of the Dead: A Prison Diary. New York: Doubleday and Co., 1974.

Prison Poems. Greensboro, N.C.: Unicorn Press, 1973.

Selected and New Poems. Garden City, N.Y.: Doubleday, 1973.

No Bars to Manhood (especially ''Open Sesame: My Life and Good Times.'') Garden City, New York: Doubleday, 1970.

And many others.

ABOUT DANIEL BERRIGAN

Deedy, John. *'Apologies, Good Friends,' An Interim Biography of Daniel Berrigan, S.J.* Mystic, Conn: Twenty-Third Publications, 1981.

du Plessix Gray, Francine. *Divine Disobedience.* New York: Random House, 1969.

Klejment, Anne. *The Berrigans: A Bibliography of Published Works by Daniel, Philip, and Elizabeth McAlister Berrigan.* New York: Garland Publishing Co., 1979.

FRANCES CROWE

1919-

"PRISON IS ANOTHER PART OF THE WORK I AM ENGAGED IN TO
end the nuclear arms race," Frances Crowe said on leaving the
Adult Correctional Institution in Cranston, Rhode Island, at
midnight February 5, 1984. She had been there, in the women's
section of the prison, for thirty days following an arrest for
attempting to deliver a "Citizens' Complaint and Indictment

for War Crimes Against Humanity'' to industrialists at Electric Boat Company, builders of nuclear submarines, at nearby Quonset Point.

Frances Crowe's release, twelve hours earlier than expected, came about through the intervention of Jesse Jackson, a candidate for the Democratic nomination for president. Together they attended a peace rally immediately afterward, and the following afternoon Mrs. Crowe spoke to a meeting of the Peace and Justice Coalition, Diocese of Worcester, forty miles from the Rhode Island prison. She discussed practical activities in parishes, schools, and communities for religious people wishing to end the nuclear arms race. A month later, she joined a group of men and women, including her husband, Dr. Thomas Crowe, a retired internist, in a peace-keeping vigil on the border between Nicaragua and Honduras. Such activities on behalf of peace and justice have characterized Frances Crowe's life for the past thirty years.

An active Quaker (Society of Friends) and for many years a member of the peace education committee of the American Friends Service Committee, she is known throughout New England where she has been honored by various religious groups for her ecumenical commitment to peacemaking. In 1983, she received the John Leary Award of the New England Catholic Peace Fellowship and, prior to that, various citations in recognition of her persistent and broadly-based campaigns against war and injustice.

During the Indochina war, thousands of young men received draft counseling on the first floor of her home in Northampton, Massachusetts, a large room that tells the history of the anti-war movement through numerous posters on the wall. There, three blocks from the Smith College campus, small groups of young men, through dialogue and role-playing, sorted out moral and political questions raised by conscription, military service, and conscientious objection. After detailed discussions, over several weeks, about where each individual "drew the line," they went off to war, to prison, or to alternative service. Such counseling, unavailable to young men in many parts of the country, contributed much, eventually, to legislation ending inductions and the peacetime draft. It amounted to a long-time public education program on the dangers of conscription, which many Americans, since Daniel Webster, regard as undemocratic and militarist.

While maintaining that center, with the help of students from nearby colleges and communities, Frances Crowe carried on another "career" of legislative lobbying at regional congressional offices as well as in Washington, D.C.; supported local women's groups and fair practices toward blacks, Puerto Ricans, and other minorities in the Connecticut River Valley; and, with the president of Amherst College and hundreds of others, got arrested at Westover Air Force Base, from which supplies were shipped to Vietnam, Cambodia, and Laos in the early 1970's.

At 64 Frances Crowe has no illusions about her effect on public policy and no doubts about each individual's power to change the world. Her life and work are excellent illustrations of the fact that a person gains energy by expending it as Robert Bly once said, speaking of his early years throwing hay on a Minnesota farm.

In a statement before Judge Albert E. DeRobbio, Washington County Superior Court, South Kingstown, Rhode Island, Mrs. Crowe listed some of many activities prior to her civil disobedience at Electric Boat.

> I have worked for many years to educate myself and my community about the futility of war. I have vigiled, marched, prayed, written letters to the editor, held meetings, shown films—in other words, organized against the nuclear arms race. I have worked through all the possible legal channels to prod Congress to cut off all funds for testing, production and deployment of the nuclear submarine. I have three grown children and one grandchild and another on the way, I have had a full life, but my children and my grandchildren deserve a chance to live out their lives—as do all children and grandchildren.

As a Friend, Frances Crowe builds on a strong tradition; she stands, one might say, on the shoulders of other Quakers, such as the Grimke Sisters and Abigail Kelley Foster, abolitionists who spoke and worked for justice in the 19th century. But unlike

those women, who come down to us as persons somewhat removed from ordinary circumstances, Frances Crowe has all the
best qualities of a middle-class American homemaker: simplicity,
a wide-ranging intelligence, a quiet assurance about the giveness
of human rights, education, travel, family life, and good times.

Born in Carthage, Missouri, on May 15, 1919, Frances
Crowe came to her vocation as peacemaker gradually. After
studies at Stephens College, in Missouri, and Syracuse University, where she first met her future husband, she moved to
Western Massachusetts to attend a training center for women
going into defense work during World War II. In 1952, after
several years in New York State, she and her family returned
to the Connecticut Valley. Discovering that their second child
had been born deaf, they settled in Northampton, Massachusetts,
near the Clarke school. About that time Mrs. Crowe became
increasingly concerned about the effects of nuclear testing and
radioactivity on her children's health. In the mid-1950s, she
joined the Women's International League for Peace and Freedom, founded by Jane Addams just prior to World War I, and
SANE. Shortly thereafter, she discovered the Society of Friends,
and the American Friends Service Committee. Work on the Test
Ban Treaty in 1963 led naturally to her efforts to stop the war
in Vietnam and later to resist the manufacture and deployment
of MX missiles and ICBMs.

In accepting the Peace and Justice Award of the United
Methodist Southern New England Conference on June 6, 1983,
Frances Crowe described her pilgrimage across fifty years, from
her experience as a young girl in Carthage, "when the Methodist minister organized a vigil against compulsory ROTC in the
high school," to the present.

"There is more opportunity for each of us to make a difference now than ever before in human history," Crowe said
in 1984.

We can each find a niche, however small, in which to work.
And I believe in the power of each of us to change. I have
and I continue to. If you don't live politically you don't
live humanly and as you can see, one gets to like it; it's
a happy choice to live in opposition to the war-oriented

society. I see nothing gloomy about acting to stop the end of life on this planet. . . and we do not have to do it alone. I believe there is a spirit—life force, God—that is helping us every day.

BY FRANCES CROWE

Frances Crowe Papers. Smith College Library, Northampton, Massachusetts.

"Face It, Then Organize." In *What Will It Take to Prevent Nuclear War? Grassroots Response to Our Most Challenging Questions.* Edited by Pat Farren. Cambridge, Mass.: Schenkman Publishing Co., 1983.

GORDON ZAHN

1918-

ALTHOUGH MANY PEOPLE REFER TO THE SECOND WORLD WAR
as a popular war, a surprising number of men refused, in conscience, to take up arms voluntarily or involuntarily. Reliable
estimates indicate that war resisters numbered about 60,000
between 1940 and 1945, with 12,000 conscientious objectors in
civilian public service camps throughout the United States,

between 25,000 and 50,000 noncombatants in the armed forces, and another 6,000 in federal prisons.

Gordon Zahn, for example, spent time in a public service camp for conscientious objectors under Catholic auspices at Weaver and Stoddard, New Hampshire. Stanley Kunitz, poet and editor, was a noncombatant soldier in the U.S. Army; and David Dillinger, editor and activist, and J.F. Powers, novelist and short story writer, spent time in federal prisons in Danbury, Connecticut, and Sandstone, Minnesota, respectively.

In "The Conscientious Objector," Karl Shapiro, an army sergeant in the South Pacific, spoke admiringly of his pacifist contemporaries during the Second World War whom he described as "the opposite of all armies":

> Well might the soldier kissing the hot beach
> Erupting in his face damn all your kind.
> Yet you who saved neither yourselves nor us
> Are equally with those who shed the blood
> The heroes of our cause. Your conscience is
> What we come back to in the armistice.

Shapiro may have been thinking of his friend Robert Lowell, another objector at this time, but these lines accurately describe Gordon Zahn as well.

Born in Milwaukee on August 7, 1918, Gordon Zahn went to work immediately after high school, and was in his early 20s when Congress initiated the draft in 1940 and extended it to the following year. At 24 he left for the C.O. camp in New Hampshire, the longest trip away from home up to that point in his life.

Zahn described the basis of his essentially religious commitment to pacifism in this way:

> It derived more from a personal and highly sentimental
> version of Christianity than from any formal instruction
> in Catholic theology. The product of a relatively mixed
> (and religiously inactive) household, I had very little con-
> tact with the faith into which I had been baptized as an
> infant. . . . My primary and secondary education was

> received in the public school system, a fact which may have
> contributed more than anything else to my [draft refusal].
> After all, had I been exposed to a parochial school train-
> ing and education, chances are good that I would have gone
> off to war like most of their other products.

Among the educated Catholics whom Zahn met at the
C.O. camp, several came from the Catholic Worker movement,
an anarchist and pacifist community that he was unfamiliar with
until that moment. Although Zahn's co-religionists regarded his
humanitarian Catholicism as unorthodox, they influenced the
direction of his later life as a student and scholar. After the war,
he studied at St. John's University in Collegeville, Minnesota,
and later at St. Thomas College in St. Paul; in 1952, he completed a Ph.D. degree in sociology at Catholic University, where
he studied with Reverend Paul Hanley Furfey, a scholar sympathetic to the Christian nonviolent tradition.

Since the time of St. Augustine, the Catholic Church's
position on war has been defined principally as the so-called just
war theory. That theory, with its origins in the era of Constantine and the Holy Roman Empire, argues that Catholics can
make war as long as the proper conditions apply; that is, if the
war is declared by a proper authority; and if the intention is right,
the cause is just, and the good achieved outweighs the evils
involved. Zahn argues, however, that modern warfare fails to
meet these conditions, and that obliteration bombing, which
breaks down any distinction between combatant and noncombatant, makes almost every condition of the just war theory
inapplicable.

Ironically, Zahn's Christian pacifism provoked arguments among the Benedictine monks at St. John's University,
and he was denied admission to the college as a sophomore. Now
generally regarded, with Thomas Merton, as a major influence
on Catholic social thought, Zahn has since been honored by the
university that sent him down as a freshman. For many years
a teacher at Loyola University, Chicago, and now professor
emeritus, University of Massachusetts, Boston, he directs the
Pax Christi Center for Law and Conscience, Cambridge, Massachusetts, and lectures widely for Pax Christi, an international

peace organization that numbers many Catholic bishops in its membership.

Two of Zahn's books have been particularly influential on American Catholics, a religious constituency once regarded as reactionary on peace issues: *German Catholics and Hitler's Wars* (1962), a study of the church's complicity with the Nazis before and during the Second World War; and *In Solitary Witness: The Life and Death of Franz Jagerstatter* (1964), about an Austrian peasant who was executed by the Germans for refusing on religious grounds to wear an army uniform. The first book was frequently cited by those who regarded America's war against Vietnam, like Germany's war against Europe, as unjust. Draftees who refused on religious grounds to cooperate with conscription frequently cited testimony from the second book. In 1968, for example, James Harney, a young seminarian, wrote that "today Jagerstatter offers courage to men who oppose a tradition of the Just War. . . which lauds the marriage between Church and State."

Zahn's story of Jagerstatter's resistance to Hitler has continued to influence Catholic social teaching. Isolated and alone against the power of church and state, that simple, uneducated man redeemed evil times by his conscientious dissent. Through such informed and unpretentious scholarship, as well as his personal witness, Zahn has helped to reclaim a tradition of Christian pacifism for contemporary activists and historians; and the American Catholic bishops, in their pastoral condemning of nuclear weapons, *The Challenge of Peace: God's Promise and Our Response* (1982), cite his work and testimony.

In an afterword to *War or Peace? The Search for New Answers* (1980), a volume of essays in his honor, Zahn provides a useful survey of the church's changing perspective on Christian pacifism:

> Twenty years ago no one of Bryan Hehir's stature would have been willing to recognize pacifism as an acceptable, much less equal, option for the Catholic. Very few Catholic writers would have given serious thought to nonviolence as a possible alternative to war, and few of these would have thought favorably of its prospects. Conscientious

objection. . . had been all but condemned by Pius XII in his 1956 Christmas message. Today we can not only cite supportive passages in the documents of Vatican Council II and in pastoral statements issued by national hierarchies, but the American bishops have gone beyond these to call for recognition of *selective* conscientious objection, and, more amazing still, amnesty for conscientious deserters of the Vietnam era. Individual bishops have appeared before courts and draft boards to plead the cause of conscientious objectors and war resisters.

For Zahn, this reversal of form borders on the miraculous. Supernatural intervention may indeed have prompted such a reversal, but historians of American Catholicism point to more clearly observable causes, including the life and writings of Gordon Zahn.

By Gordon Zahn

Another Part of the War: The Camp Simon Story. Amherst: University of Massachusetts Press, 1979.

German Catholics and Hitler's Wars: A Study in Social Control. New York: Sheed and Ward, 1962, and New York: E.P. Dutton, 1969.

War, Conscience and Dissent. New York: Hawthorne Books, Inc., 1967.

In Solitary Witness: The Life and Death of Franz Jägerstatter. New York: Holt, Rinehart, and Winston, 1964; Boston: Beacon Press, 1968; and Collegeville, Minn.: Liturgical Press, 1980. *The Refusal,* a film based upon the Jägerstatter story is available from Pax Christi USA, 6227 W. Cornelia, Chicago, Illinois 60634.

And others.

About Gordon Zahn

War or Peace?: The Search for New Answers. Edited by Thomas A. Shannon. Maryknoll, New York: Orbis Books, 1980.

ANNABEL WOLFSON

1915-1983

ALTHOUGH ONE SELDOM HEARS CITIZENSHIP CALLED AN ART, Annabel Kreider Wolfson gave that ordinary station great distinction.

A true democrat who held no political or ecclesiastical office, she embodied the qualities that Paine, Jefferson, and the 18th century philosophers associated with enlightened men and women: respect for the Common Law, the vote, civil liberties, and the rule of reason. She believed, with Paul Goodman, that "we have no right to surrender our inheritance to boors and tyrants."

In a less barbarous age, Annabel Wolfson would have been widely recognized for her wisdom, perhaps as an adviser to governments and presidents. As it was, she found herself in opposition to them—to war, to conscription, and to the imperial policies of the United States since World War II. Unlike many of us, who become discouraged or cynical about prospects for change, she worked persistently and selflessly for a better world, and sometimes, surprisingly enough, she got it.

It was partly through her efforts, for example, that the Selective Service System stopped drafting young men in 1973. By then "peacetime" conscription had been on the books for a quarter of a century. Testifying for draft repeal in 1971, before the Senate Armed Services Committee, Mrs. Wolfson said: "Any selective system of choosing men for compulsory military service is inherently unfair. The present Selective Service System is unfair in its administration as well."

As a volunteer counselor to thousands of young men of draft age, she understood the inequities of the draft better than most people. In this area of citizenship, Annabel Wolfson was the voice for many who could not or would not openly oppose military conscription. In the words of a lawyer who depended upon her expert advice in cases before the courts: "If all of us spoke out the way that she did, the world would be in better shape than it's in."

Born in Harrisburg, Pennsylvania, on October 30, 1915, and educated in public schools there, Annabel Kreider studied nursing at Mount Sinai Hospital, in New York, where she met her husband, Dr. Irving Wolfson. In the 1950s, they moved to central Massachusetts, where their children grew up and where Mrs. Wolfson was active on the board of the public library, a volunteer coordinator for UNICEF, and co-founder and principal adviser to the Interfaith Center for Draft Information.

Her special love was language, and her liturgy—like that of the church she grew up in—was the liturgy of the word. Readings and hymns selected by her for a memorial service, at the Unitarian/Universalist Church in Worcester, included verses of William Cullen Bryant and Walter Chalmers Smith. She identified, in other words, with that wing of Protestantism long associated with social reform. It is a noble tradition in American culture, with links to the abolitionist movement in the 19th century and to various peace and justice movements of the 20th century.

Although she cared little for music or painting, Mrs. Wolfson had read more novels than anyone I have ever known, and remembered details and recounted stories from most of them. Tolerant of anyone whose knowledge was less specific than her own, she unknowingly made one feel ignorant nonetheless on a wide range of subjects: fiction, gardening, home repairs, law, medicine, child care, and the voting records of most members of congress. Over the years, she kept her representatives, as well as her friends, informed on the implications of proposed legislation. For that reason, she created something of a stir in congressional offices in Washington during occasional visits.

Although a bit shy about speaking in public, Mrs. Wolfson wrote letters to the editor of local newspapers and participated in radio talk shows. Her attention to precise details on many subjects came from her wide experience as a nurse, mother, citizen, as well as from her reading the daily New York *Times,* the *Congressional Record,* and various publications associated with public issues.

Her commitment to the regional Interfaith Center for Draft Information was representative of her faithful service. Initiated in 1969, with support from the Worcester County Ecumenical Council, the Roman Catholic Diocese, and the Jewish Federation, the ICDI enables young men to make informed decisions about the draft, and provides assistance as well to guidance counselors, clergy, lawyers, teachers, and parents. Although there are many trained counselors in New England, almost no one possessed her comprehensive knowledge of the draft laws and regulations.

But Annabel Wolfson's work with the draft was merely one manifestation of her commitment to an informed citizenry. From 1962-1983, for example, she helped to raise approximately $80,000 for UNICEF, to feed and clothe the world's children.

Her presence in the community amounted to a kind of ministry to needs that many so-called professions only pretend to address. As a "teacher," she put most college professors to shame in her ability to make her learning available to others. To work with her was to absorb what she knew almost without realizing it.

At the center of Annabel Wolfson's being was a humanity, a reverence for life, that was deep, intelligent, and disinterested. The main character in *Henderson the Rain King* (1959) by Saul Bellow, one of her favorite writers, makes two statements that might have been hers: "The forgiveness of sins is perpetual and righteousness first is not required," Henderson says at one point. And the other: "Whatever gains I ever made were always due to love and nothing else." Although she was too ironic to speak directly about such weighty matters, she lived the values implied in these maxims.

About the rearing of children, she was more direct. Once asked how to teach good moral values to young people, she responded without hesitation: "Children must be taught to be honest. And I don't mean just with money. Many people are inclined to do something for convenience's sake, when it should be done another way."

By Annabel Wolfson's example and at her insistence, many people learned to live as responsible citizens, with the attendant rights, duties, and responsibilities. Because of her, others now work to sustain the life-giving services that she valued, and to practice the art of citizenship that she performed so effectively in her community.

BY ANNABEL WOLFSON

"A Matter of Spending Priorities." Worcester (Mass.) *Evening Gazette,* March 1, 1972.

MURIEL RUKEYSER

1913-1980

SHE HAD COME BY TRAILWAYS BUS TO WORCESTER, MASSACHU-setts, in May 1974, where she was to give a poetry reading at the public library that very evening. In New York, the night before, she had attended a performance of *Ulysses in Nighttown,* a dramatization of the last section of Joyce's novel. Shortly after the bus pulled up to the curb, Muriel Rukeyser moved haltingly down the steps of the bus, looking as if she had been jostled by a crowd of shoppers. Her hair, thin and graying, was in disarray; she wore dark fabric slippers, resembling ballet shoes, and her stockings sagged a bit below the black dress that hung unevenly just below the knees. Although she looked rather confused, she spoke the moment she recognized me, saying, ''I haven't quite recovered yet from the play. The Molly Bloom soliloquy was so powerful—her story is every woman's story.''

Two years later a friend of mine met her on a similar occasion. She told him she had heard a woman (while pointing to her on the bus) say to her daughter, ''Isn't that the worst looking woman you ever saw?''

Such memories remain, in part, because they conflict so decidedly with Muriel Rukeyser's appearance on stage, where she was a commanding, a noble presence. She read her remarkable poems in a clear, deep voice, in the grand manner, and the times I heard her she maintained complete command of the audience. There, as in private conversation, one was reminded of the young woman whose early photographs showed her to be strikingly beautiful, with large dark eyes, black hair styled in the 19th century manner, above a full, olive-colored face. She was conscious of her beauty, and the illnesses in later life and the increased weight troubled her and shook her confidence.

I think of her, also, as she was photographed in 1975, in Seoul, Korea; she stood in the rain outside a prison, reading a statement on behalf of the poet Kim Chi Ha, a political prisoner under the military government there. Threatened with execution for his courageous defense of others, Kim Chi Ha is alive today partly as a result of Rukeyser's efforts, the support of Amnesty International and PEN. She had been involved in similar struggles ever since her journey to Alabama as a college sophomore in 1933 to cover the Scottsboro Boys Trial, when it was ''illegal'' to do so. And she spent time in jail in Manhattan and in Washington D.C., later, in support of draft resisters and in civil disobedience against the nuclear arms race. Even after two strokes in her mid-60s, prior to her death in February 1980, Rukeyser traveled and worked for social justice, particularly during her tenure as president of PEN, the international organization of poets, essayists, and novelists.

A member of a wealthy Philadelphia family, she was born in New York City on December 15, 1913, educated at experimental schools there and at Vassar College (with Mary McCarthy, Elizabeth Bishop, and Eleanor Clark). Shortly after leaving college she learned to fly a plane, and then turned to film editing, photography, traveling, and wrote for various periodicals. In 1935, she received the Yale Younger Poets Award for her first collection, *Theory of Flight.* Among her well-known early poems are "Boy with His Hair Cut Short," about a young man looking for work during the Depression, and "The Lynchings of Jesus" in which she said of the young black men, in the famous Scottsboro Boys Trial: "Dred Scott wrestles for freedom there in the corner/ All our celebrated troubles are repeated here."

In 1936 she went to England and, eventually, to Spain to cover the People's Olympiad, an alternative to the Olympic Games being held in Berlin. The beginning of the Spanish Civil War gave her, as it gave George Orwell, a positive view of social change: "Even the gypsies on the docks in Barcelona were with this. It was a curious vision of a 20th century world which would not take place," she said later.

An assignment in the graphics division of the Office of War Information during World War II ended after only six months when, along with Ben Shahn and others, Rukeyser began to portray the deeper implications of the war. From there she moved to San Francisco, where she taught at the California Labor School, married, and gave birth to her only child, a son. At that time, she helped to initiate public poetry readings that contributed to the San Francisco Renaissance. Returning to New York in 1954, she taught at Sarah Lawrence College and was subsequently elected to the National Institute of Arts and Letters.

During the 1960s, Rukeyser gave benefit readings for the antiwar movement, and in 1972, she traveled on a peace mission to Hanoi with Denise Levertov and Jane Hart. The women's movement and two excellent films about her life and work gradually enlarged the audience for her poetry, even as failing health caused a curtailment of a busy schedule of readings, teaching, and writing in her last years and until her death in 1980.

Rukeyser's poetry reflects her strong sense of the common lot of ordinary people—their suffering, their work, their confusion in the midst of a sometimes cruel and awkward century. It is that consciousness of pain and her powerful rendering of that awareness that give her poetry its prophetic quality. Though written in some cases almost half a century ago, what she wrote seems especially current. The later poems, especially *The Speed of Darkness* (1968), about people out of work, about failures of communication between lovers, are among the truly memorable lyrics of the period.

In her life and in her thirty books of fiction, poetry, and translations, Rukeyser was constantly striking out toward new territories. She did so not merely to rebel against convention, but in order to alert others to the peculiar tensions of the moment. This penchant for the unexpected kept her readers alert and critics perpetually confused, so it will be some years before literary history and criticism attend to her achievements. In the meantime, the common reader, the one responsible for her present audience, keeps her work visible. I have never called her poems to the attention of readers and students without them responding with extraordinary enthusiasm.

Rukeyser was not a ''thinker,'' and her writings sometimes sound rhetorical rather than analytical. Her language is the language of song. She seems not to speak to the immediate hurt or social concern, the way a more conventional writer would, but provides, one might say, something more essential: a psychological grounding for a private or political truth. One can only guess at the depth of suffering on her part that is at the base of such understanding. The strength at the heart of these insights is the reason, no doubt, that her poetry is both sustaining and lasting. Here is one example:

Poem

I lived in the first century of world wars.
Most mornings I would be more or less insane,
The newspapers would arrive with their careless stories,
The news would pour out of various devices
Interrupted by attempts to sell products to the unseen.
I would call my friends on other devices;
They would be more or less mad for similar reasons.

Slowly I would get to pen and paper,
Make my poems for others unseen and unborn.
In the day I would be reminded of those men and women
Brave, setting up signals across the vast distances,
Considering a nameless way of living, of almost un-
    imagined values.
As the lights darkened, as the lights of night bright-
    ened,
We would try to imagine them, try to find each other.
To construct peace, to make love, to reconcile
Waking with sleeping, ourselves with each other.
Ourselves with ourselves. We would try by any means
To reach the limits of ourselves, to reach beyond
    ourselves,
To let go the means, to wake.
I lived in the first century of these wars.

BY MURIEL RUKEYSER

The Collected Poems. New York: McGraw Hill Co., 1978.

The Life of Poetry. New York: William Morrow and Co., (1949), 1974.

"Craft Interview with Muriel Rukeyser." In *The Craft of Poetry.* Edited by William Packard. Garden City, New York: Doubleday, 1974.

And others.

ABOUT MURIEL RUKEYSER

Kertesz, Louise. *The Poetic Vision of Muriel Rukeyser.* Baton Rouge: Louisiana State University Press, 1980.

MULFORD SIBLEY

1912-

"THE CONFRONTATIONS OF OUR DAY RAISE MANY QUESTIONS,"
Mulford Sibley wrote fifteen years ago, both among those who
challenge the existing structure and among those who rule. For
the first group, the issues include "the meaning of conscience,
the nature of obligation, and the purposes of disobedience," and
for the second, "the justification for repression, the inherent

limitations of the law, and the inertia of institutions.''

Across four decades, in essays, books, and pamphlets, including *The Obligation to Disobey* (1970), Professor Sibley has provided the most useful body of writings on the politics of pacifism since Gandhi. In the meantime, he has maintained an active, even famous career as a teacher of political theory and as a civil libertarian and war resister.

Born in Marston, Missouri, on June 14, 1912, Mulford Q. Sibley grew up in Oklahoma, graduating from Central State University, Edmund, and the university in Norman in the mid-thirties; in 1938, he completed a doctorate in political science at the University of Minnesota. After teaching for ten years at the University of Illinois, he returned to Minneapolis/St. Paul, and has taught at colleges and universities there, and throughout the United States and abroad. His other longtime associations include the American Service Committee and the Martin Luther King Institute of Nonviolent Social Change in Atlanta, which he advises.

In the Upper Midwest, Sibley is something of a legend as a teacher and Socialist. His debate with a St. Paul alderman in the late 1960s about who should or should not be allowed to espouse what causes on a state university campus attracted audiences throughout the region; it raised basic questions about the relationship between the university and the community among the general public, as well as among scholars and students throughout the United States.

The significance and originality of Sibley's political thought is best suggested by one of his earliest pamphlets, *The Political Theories of Modern Pacifism: An Analysis and Criticism* (1944), which contains both a summary of modern pacifist thought and a critique of its major arguments ''insofar as they related themselves to the world of politics.''

It describes the philosophical bases of Hindu pacifism, Christian pacifism, and the pacifism of the secular revolutionary movements of the 19th and 20th centuries, and then evaluates several main currents or propositions that all pacifist theories hold in common. Among them are (1) that violence hinders the achievement of a democratic and peaceful order; (2) that decentralization in politics and in the economic order is desirable; and

(3) that the ideology of nonviolence has a direct relevance to politics. The last two tenets provide modern pacifism with its greatest challenge, if, that is, it is to deal with questions that go beyond personal witness.

In showing how pacifism speaks to these concerns, Sibley prefers Gandhi's theory of politics to that of the Christian anarchists, secularists, or other utopians of the last two centuries, particularly regarding the State. "While the pacifist is right in protesting against the swallowing up of the individual personality by the Leviathan State," overemphasizing decentralization and agrarianism raises problems, too, he says. "A world in which the binding tie of political cohesion is practically severed would be a poor setting for social harmony and nonviolence."

Like Gandhi and unlike the anarchists, Sibley regards maintenance of the State as compatible with a pacifist ethic; and he argues against those, such as the late Reinhold Niebuhr, who say pacifism has no direct relevance to modern politics. It may, in fact, be "the only context in which to discover the road to a new polity," Sibley argues. "In this respect Hindu and secular revolutionary pacifism are far more penetrating than most emphases of Christian pacifism." Gandhi, for example, whose political theory involved a philosophy of history, a doctrine of the ideal State, as well as a theory of revolution, saw that in any mass action previous agreement is essential, "if the power of the State is to be effectively challenged."

It is against this background—providing a theoretical basis for a new politics based upon nonviolence—that Sibley's work is best understood, including his later discussions of *power, authority,* and *violence.* These concepts, as Hannah Arendt also has argued, must be clarified if one is to deal with the crucial issue in politics, Who rules whom?

In considering various sides of this question, including those related to civil disobedience, Sibley calls upon a fund of knowledge of past nonviolent resistance—from his own book, *The Quiet Battle* (1968), as well as from the Civil Rights and anti-war movements and resistance to the nuclear arms race. He often supports an argument by reference to alternative or "revolutionary" practices, such as resisting conscription and war taxes, hiding political prisoners (Jews in Germany, for example, during

World War II), and exposing secret government war agreements.

Sibley recognizes at the same time the hazards that continue to make the application of the pacifist principles difficult "in a world that is more violent and less free" than it was forty years ago. He wrote in *The Obligation to Disobey:*

> In attempting to make ends and means compatible with each other, the pacifist is both a revolutionary and a political realist. Only radical social reconstruction can provide a framework which will encourage respect for human personality. But peace cannot be attained by war, and reverence for human beings will not be advanced by methods deliberately meant to kill and maim them . . . .
> Only when radicals emancipate themselves from the fatal fascination which violence still apparently has for them can they become leaders in the cause of equalitarian revolution.

As political theory, the writings of Mulford Sibley deserve serious study by everyone who works for fundamental social change. As a scholar, teacher, and "quiet battler" in his own right, Sibley has helped to lay the groundwork for a radical culture. In his own life, also, he provides a vivid example of the necessary relationship between political theory and practices between the politics of pacifism and nonviolent direct action.

Sibley has been an especially popular teacher, admired even by those not particularly sympathetic to his pacifist and socialist politics. For forty years his tall, lanky figure was almost as much of an institution as the Mississippi River that cuts through the University of Minnesota campus, where he taught seminars on Plato and Marx, general courses in Medieval political thought and political theory, and served as adviser to the program in American Studies.

Now a lecturer at Hamline University and Macalester College, he is known for his ability to present all sides of a question fairly, even while making clear his own position. This reputation for integrity has prompted several people, including a vice president of the United States, to come to his defense when political bureaucrats occasionally harassed him for questioning conventional behavior and publicly espousing unpopular causes.

BY MULFORD SIBLEY

The Obligation to Disobey: Conscience and the Law. New York: Council on Religion and International Affairs, 1970.

The Quiet Battle: Writings on the Theory and Practice of Non-violent Resistance. Garden City, N.Y.: Doubleday, 1963 and Boston: Beacon Press, 1968.

The Political Theories of Modern Pacifism: An Analysis and Criticism. Philadelphia: The Pacifist Research Bureau, 1944, 1970.

And others.

ABOUT MULFORD SIBLEY

Morphew, Clark. "Peace Prof: Controversial Ideas Still Propel Mulford Q. Sibley." St. Paul (Minn.) *Post Dispatch* (March 3, 1984), pp. 1B-2B.

PAUL GOODMAN

1911-1972

PAUL GOODMAN'S LAY SERMON TO THE NATIONAL SECURITY
Industrial Association in 1967 repeated the decentralist and libertarian arguments of his pamphlets and poems. While thirty
students picketed and leafletted the auditorium on the outside,
Goodman read the riot act to the militarists and industrialists
on the inside:

You are unfitted by your commitments, your experience, your customary methods, your recruitment, and your moral disposition to provide research and development for the socioeconomic environment of the 1970s (the theme of the conference). You are the military industrial of the United States, the most dangerous body of men at the present in the world, for you not only implement our disastrous policies but are an overwhelming lobby for them, and you expand and rigidify the wrong use of brains, resources, and labor so that change becomes difficult. Most likely the trends you represent will be interrupted by a shambles of riots, alienation, ecological catastrophes, wars, and revolutions, so that current long-range planning, including this conference, is irrelevant.

The best service that you people could render is rather rapidly to phase yourselves out, passing on your relevant knowledge to people better qualified or reorganizing yourselves with entirely different sponsors and commitments, so that you learn to think and feel in a different way. Since you are most of the Research and Development that there is, we cannot do without you as people, but we cannot do with you as you are.

This unique perspective and approach to a contemporary problem was characteristically *ad hominem,* direct, moralistic, and practical, drawing upon his experience as philosopher, poet, novelist, teacher, and literary critic.

Although he began writing in the 30s, Paul Goodman belongs to the 1960s in a peculiar and significant way. Educated during the Depression, where he learned the good things that the angry decade had to teach, he served as a kind of perpetual faculty adviser to young men and women discovering American radicalism during the civil rights and antiwar movements thirty years later. Student manifestos were sometimes little more than paraphrases of his pamphlets, and from 1959 until his death, he was a frequent participant in seminars, teach-ins, institutes, and conferences such as the one in Washington, D.C., described above. As an anarchist who survived the Cold War of the 50s with his politics intact, he understood a great deal about the implications of resistance and about "drawing the line" (the title of one of his pamphlets, published in 1962).

Goodman gave strength and guidance to various movements for social change in the 60s, by his presence and his popular magazine articles; that decade also made him a success, a household word. His best poems and essays, especially *Growing Up Absurd* (1960), belong to that period when his paperback books sold thousands of copies a week. Although this popularity did not increase his personal happiness, he thrived on it as a writer, since he needed a large and appreciative public to work well. He was almost fifty before his books won the audience they deserved, and *Five Years* (his only bad book) records the pain that isolation during the middle years caused him.

As a social critic, he was not corrupted by success:

> Despite the alleged temptation, I do not find that being a well-known author and being called on for public speeches has reconciled me to the American way of life. Our establishment does not improve on closer acquaintance. One advantage of being a "success" is that I can now say my say without being accused of sour grapes.

As an artist, Goodman was an urban Thoreau: *Communitas* (1947), a meditation on city planning, was his *Walden;* the Hudson River, his Walden Pond; and he preached a moral remarkably similar to that of the Concord transcendentalist: "Simplify, simplify, simplify." A characteristic sentence, beautiful in strength, perception, and good-old American bawdy and backwoods humor, summarizes his utopian proposals: "I have learned to have very modest goals for society and myself, things like clean air and water, green grass, children with bright eyes, not being pushed around, useful work that suits one's abilities, plain tasty food, and occasional satisfactory nookie."

His attitude toward social change is summarized in the prefaces to two books. The first, from *Compulsory Miseducation* (1964), describes the waste of money and people in the American school system and the lack of new ideas:

> It is uncanny. When, at a meeting, I offer that perhaps

we already have too much formal schooling. . . . the others
look at me oddly. . . . I realize suddenly that I am confronting a mass superstition, as well as an objective fact:

> Major conditions of modern life *are* unprecedented and we
> do not know how to cope with them. Confused, people
> inevitably try to ward off anxiety by rigidifying the old
> methods of dominant economic and intellectual groups.

Supporting his own argument by reference to an underlying
psychological condition, Goodman manages to surround the
topic, to occupy the territory above and below. It is a favorite
ploy, in the best analytic and didactic tradition, fast-moving,
dazzling and convincing.

Similarly, in the preface to *The Society I Live in Is Mine*
(1962), a gathering of fugitive essays and letters to the editor,
Goodman speaks of deteriorating citizenship in a society that
should be open to individual voices and initiatives.

> It is appalling how few people regard themselves as citizens,
> as society makers. Instead they regard society as a pre-
> established machinery of institutions and authorities and
> they take themselves as I don't know what, some kind of
> individuals 'in' society, whatever that means. Such a view
> is dangerous because it must result in a *few* people being
> society makers and exercising power over the rest. . . .
> The result must be and has been stupid standardization,
> stupid neglect, stupid injustice, and a base common
> denominator of valuation. There is no remedy except large
> numbers of authentic citizens, alert, concerned, interven-
> ing, deciding on all issues and all levels.

In poetry, Goodman exhibited a strong, if sometimes
careless talent for lyricism. To the end, Goodman regarded
himself as a traditionalist, a child of the Reformation (Luther
and Milton) and the Enlightenment (Kant and Jefferson), and
a classicist. Such a prodigous and impressive patrimony might
seem pretentious when claimed by most writers. But Goodman
wore the mantle lightly, and he made his immense learning
available, useful, and exciting to any who wished to share it.

A native New Yorker, where he was born in 1911, Good-man attended City College and Columbia University before com-pleting his Ph.D. at the University of Chicago. Returning to New York, where he stayed most of the rest of his life, he and his family lived in poverty until about 1960. He often carried his essays to magazine editors by bicycle, to save on postage. The death of a son and ill-health during his last years caused him much unhappiness, and the revised versions of his essays lack the strength and vitality of the original versions. Yet up to the end, even shortly before his death in New Hampshire in 1972, he kept reminding people of a potentially beautiful, reasonable, and erotic world and arguing practically as well as theoretically how to bring it into being. The logic, the rhetoric of his writings, "the dumb-bunny alternatives," as he called them, suggest what the reader might *do* about the confusion and oppression, and Goodman's best essays are among the liveliest and most original writing on education, religion and language—on humane living—that we have.

BY PAUL GOODMAN

Collected Poems. Edited by Taylor Stoehr. New York: Random House, 1973.

The Community of Scholars. New York: Random House, 1964.

Compulsory Miseducation. New York: Random House, 1962.

Drawing the Line. (rev.) New York: Random House, 1962.

The Society I Love in Is Free. New York: Horizon Books, 1962.

Communitias: Means of Livelihood and Ways of Life, with Percival Good-man. New York: Random House, 1960.

Growing Up Absurd. New York: Random House, 1956.

And others.

ABOUT PAUL GOODMAN

King, Richard. *The Party of Eros: Radical Social Thought in the Realm of Freedom.* Chapel Hill: University of North Carolina Press, 1972.

Nicely, Tom. "Notes Toward a Bibliography." In *The Writings of Paul Goodman, New Letters,* No. 2 and 3 (1976), 246-53.

Roszak, Theodore. *Making of a Counter Culture.* New York: Doubleday and Co., 1969.

HANNAH ARENDT

1906-1976

EVEN HANNAH ARENDT'S CRITICS, AT THE TIME OF HER DEATH IN 1976, generally agreed that she was one of America's foremost political philosophers. But William Barrett's description of her mind as "something of an eighth wonder" was perhaps more to the point.

It was a distinction achieved through a life of considerable

suffering, from the early death of her father through her displace-
ment as a German Jew, first to Paris in the 1930s and then to
the United States. In America, her talent and courage were tested
once again when she had to face critics who almost wilfully
misread her books, particularly the controversial study, *Eichmann
in Jerusalem: A Report on the Banality of Evil* (1963). An analysis
of the catastrophe of Nazi Germany, it demonstrated the inade-
quacy of the legel system to deal with "the facts of administrative
massacres organized by the state apparatus." Like Orwell's *Nineteen Eighty-Four,* it was a warning to all, not just an expose' of an
isolated case; and some commentators resented her scrupulous
honesty in telling the story of those complicit in the destruction
of the Jews.

Hannah Arendt was elegant, even aristocratic in manner and style. Although many of her books and essays were
initially written in German, her later informal essays read as
if they were written by someone native to American English.
Two memorable sayings, slightly paraphrased, suggest something
of the depth and liveliness of her thought:

> (1) One must remember that in choosing the lesser of two
> evils one still chooses evil; (2) And if you can't laugh away
> the learned and sophisticated rubbish about 'adjustment'
> to one's environment, what help is there? To disprove point
> by point all the nonsense our century has produced would
> demand ten life spans, and in the end the disprovers would
> be indistinguishable from the victims.

Born in Hannover, Germany, on October 14, 1906, Hannah Arendt studied at the universities of Marburg and Freiburg
and at Heidelberg where, at 22, she received a Ph.D. in
philosophy, minoring in theology and Greek. At Heidelberg,
she studied with Karl Jaspers and Martin Heidegger, whose work
she later edited, and wrote a dissertation on St. Augustine. With
the rise of Hitler, she fled to Paris in 1933, working among other
Jewish refugees, and finally to New York. Her thirty-year
marriage to Heinrich Bluchner was a happy one, as were her
friendships with various writers, including W.H. Auden, who
once proposed to her; Randall Jarrell, who read poetry to her;

and Mary McCarthy, who edited Arendt's posthumously published volumes, *The Life of the Mind: Thinking, Willing, and Judging* (1978).

Before being named a full professor at Princeton in 1959 (the first woman to hold that position), Arendt worked as an editor and administrator in New York. Later she taught at other leading universities, including the University of Chicago and, at the time of her death, at the New School for Social Research.

In returning to several of her writings, one is struck by how indispensable each of them remains: *The Origins of Totalitarianism* (1951), on the Russian and German political scenes during the 20th century; *The Human Condition* (1958), on three fundamental human activities of labor, work, and action; and the revised edition of *Eichmann in Jerusalem,* in which she answers her various critics.

Among the other books, *Crisis of the Republic* (1972) deserves special attention by anyone active in justice issues, because of its discussions of nonviolent direct action and of fundamental social change. It includes a careful analysis of the successes and failures of student radicalism in the 1960s, defining for contemporary culture such terms as *power, authority, force,* and *violence.* "Out of the barrel of a gun grows the most effective command resulting in the most instant and perfect obedience," Arendt says (challenging the Maoist doctrine). "What never can grow out of it is power." She regarded the concept of civil disobedience as a peculiarly American phenomenon, related to other political institutions. "In contrast to the conscientious objector, the civil disobedient is a member of a group, whether we like it or not, founded in accordance with the same spirit that has formed voluntary associations."

Among her more popular writings were the telling portraits of John XXIII and Berthold Brecht, in *Men in Dark Times* (1968). In all of her writings, for the general reader as well as for the scholar, she is concerned with education, which she defined as "a preparation for the task of renewing a common world."

A persistent theme in Arendt's writings is the realtionship between private matters—a philosopher's language, for example—and public affairs. The philosopher, she says in *Men in Dark Times,* "resembles the statesman, in that he must answer for his opinions." She recognized and fulfilled that responsibility in a special way, continually testing her thought against the major issues of her time. Although she was extremely knowledgeable about the past (she taught seminars on Plato and Aristotle), there was no doubt in the reader's mind as to what century she lived in. (With most academics, one is never sure.) As she once said to Karl Jaspers, her mentor, indicating a fundamental conviction of her life, both philosophy and politics concern everyone.

Such a position led Arendt to make rather pointed criticisms of her academic colleagues and of earlier philosophers. In "Martin Heidegger at Eighty," about her mentor, she wrote, for example: "We who wish to honor him . . . can hardly help finding it striking and perhaps exasperating that Plato and Heidegger, when they entered into human affairs, turned to tyrants and Fuhrers."

Although she loved the United States and its political traditions, she spoke out vigorously against what she saw as the corruption of language and thought in contemporary politics, especially during the Nixon administration. She said in *Crises of the Republic,*

> The quicksand of lying statements of all sorts, deceptions as well as self-deceptions, is apt to engulf any reader who wishes to probe *[The Pentagon Papers]* which, unhappily, one must recognize as the infrastructure of nearly a decade of United States foreign and domestic policy.

Arendt hoped nonetheless that the United States might still regain its integrity. It became clear to her in 1971, she said, that "the halfhearted attempts of the government to circumvent constitutional guarantees and to intimidate those who have made up their minds not to be intimidated, who would rather go to jail than see their liberties nibbled away, are not enough and probably will not be enough to destroy the Republic."

As a philosopher knowledgeable about the harsh realities of contemporary politics, Hannah Arendt made unique contributions to modern social thought. Her writings and her life carry always the mark of true humanity, suggesting that thought and language have consequences and that, even in dark times, reason has a chance.

By Hannah Arendt

Crises of the Republic: Lying in Politics, Civil Disobedience, On Violence, Thoughts or Politics, and Revolution. New York: Harcourt Brace Jovenovich, 1972.

Men in Dark Times. New York: Harcourt Brace and World, 1968.

Eichmann in Jerusalem: A Report on the Banality of Evil. New York: The Viking Press, 1963, 1964.

The Origins of Totalitarianism. Cleveland: World Publishing Company, 1951, 1966.

And others.

About Hannah Arendt

Young-Bruehl, Elizabeth. *Hannah Arendt: For Love of the World.* New Haven: Yale University Press, 1982.

STANLEY KUNITZ

1905-

THE MOST LIBERATING IDEA IN STANLEY KUNITZ'S WRITING, ONE
that allies him forever with those who work for justice in an unjust
world, builds on Albert Camus' statement that a writer, by definition, must serve not those who make history, but those who are
subject to it. To this Kunitz adds in ''Poet and State'' that a
contemporary artist must realize that he lives at a time when

"some refusals are no longer permitted him, lest he wither at the heart." "To whom can one pledge one's allegiance," he asks conclusively, "except to the victims?"

An obvious example of Kunitz's faithfulness to that pledge is his achievement as an artist. But as a conscientious objector during the Second World War, he upheld that value in his private life as well.

Drafted into the army in 1943, at the age of thirty-eight, Kunitz agreed to serve, but only on the condition that he not bear arms. At that point, the nightmare began. For months, he was moved from camp to camp to dig latrines and to perform other menial tasks, as a punishment for his refusal to carry weapons. Only after he was shipped to a base in North Carolina, where with a group of black soldiers he edited a weekly army news magazine called *Ten Minute Break,* was he treated with some decency. A published poet and a successful editor, just barely young enough to be drafted, he was eventually offered a commission, which he refused, and spent the final months of the war in an office in Washington, D.C.

Yet out of that dark time came the impetus for one of Kunitz's finest poems, "Around Pastor Bonhoeffer," written twenty years later. The subject is the well-known German theologian, Dietrich Bonhoeffer, who was, like Kunitz, caught between the violence of Hitler's war and his own conscience. A Lutheran pastor in Germany, Bonhoeffer joined the plot to kill Hitler, but only after a great struggle with his conscience. "The plot failed, and he was exterminated," Kunitz wrote later. "The conflict between his Christian principle of nonviolence and the political necessity for action seems to me a parable of our times. I myself am a nonviolent man with radical feelings about the way things are." This tension between two conflicting responsibilities undoubtedly contributes to the muted, yet haunting political reverberations in much of Kunitz's work.

Born in Worcester, Massachusetts, on July 29, 1905, the son of a Lithuanian immigrant, Stanley Kunitz never knew his father, who drowned himself a few months before his son was born, leaving his mother with three young children and many debts. In spite of these hardships, Kunitz excelled as a student in high school, where he edited the school literary magazine, as well as at Harvard University, where he completed a B.A. in 1926. His M.A. thesis, a year later, centered on the early Modernists, especially Yeats and Joyce.

In the 1930s, Kunitz published his first collection of poems, *Intellectual Things,* and edited several volumes and a bulletin for the Wilson Library company. After two years in the army in the early 1940's, he took a series of jobs as a teacher, at Bennington College, the University of Washington, and eventually at Columbia University, where he still conducts a poetry workshop for young writers. In the intervening years, he published several volumes of poetry, received various fellowships and prizes for his writing, and served as editor of the Yale Younger Poets series, 1969-77. Since 1957, he has spent half the year in Provincetown, on Cape Cod, and the other half in New York City.

Hearing his poems read aloud, one is reminded that they grew out of Kunitz's own experience of the Depression, the Second World War, the Cold War, the 60s, and after. Along the way, his persistent devotion to a high standard of performance has occasionally gone unnoticed. *Selected Poems* (1958), for example, which eventually received a Pulitzer Prize, was rejected by seven publishers.

Kunitz's politics have also complicated his life, with only a hint of that at the middle of a poem or in an autobiographical aside in his essays. In "River Road," for example, he wrote,

> My only other callers were the FBI,
> sent to investigate me as a Russian spy
> by patriotic neighbors on the river road.

As a member "of a flinty maverick line," however, he almost expects such treatment, as he said in "Journal for my Daughter:"

> In my father's time, I'm told
> our table was set in turn
> for Maxim Gorky, Emma Goldman,
> and the atheist Ingersoll

Kunitz's devotion to craft is unsparing, and his poems

are often very tough evocations of an age when, as he says in
"The Testing-Tree,"

> it is necessary to move
> through dark and deeper dark
> and not to turn.

As a writer among the crowd, he has not lost his way in the
political and moral confusion of the time; and his independence
in the midst of changing fashions of literary style has won him
the admiration of younger writers.

Gregory Orr, for example, believes that Kunitz's poetry
says to us "that the imagination, if it is courageous enough, can
triumph over the powers of desolation; that, even in our
vulnerability, we can confront the destructive element and
transform it into a wellspring, a vital source."

In his essays, Kunitz once described the work of the
imagination as "precisely what has to be achieved if we are going
to save our civilization from disaster."

By maintaining a difficult balance between innocence and
rage, Kunitz's poetry signifies the triumph of order in a chaotic
time. In a short poem called "The State," he warns his audience
also against all those who can be counted upon to do the
oppressor's "dirty work":

> That pack of scoundrels
> tumbling through the gate
> emerges
> as the Order of the State.

At 80, Stanley Kunitz sings, with grace and wit, "An Old
Cracked Tune":

> My name is Solomon Levi,
> the desert is my home,
> my mother's breast was thorny,
> and father I had none.
>
> The sands whispered, *Be separate,*

the stones taught me, *Be hard,*
I dance, for the joy of surviving,
on the edge of the road.

By Stanley Kunitz

The Poems of Stanley Kunitz, 1928-1978. Boston: Little, Brown and Company, 1979.

A Kind of Order, A Kind of Folly: Essays and Conversations. Boston: Little, Brown and Company, 1975.

And others.

About Stanley Kunitz

Henault, Marie. *Stanley Kunitz.* Boston: G.K. Hall and Company, 1980.

"On the Poetry of Stanley Kunitz." *Antaeus,* XXXVII (Spring 1980), 101-53.

GEORGE ORWELL

1903-1950

AS A YOUNG MAN, HE CALLED HIMSELF A TORY ANARCHIST, INDI-
cating both his affection for English culture and his hatred of
British imperialism. But by 1936, at 33, George Orwell identified himself as a Socialist. That was the political stance, in spite
of his persistent criticism of fellow socialists, that he respected:
the only one, he felt, that might resist the drift toward totalitar-

ianism in England and in other liberal democracies after World War II. The danger lay in the structure imposed on any country preparing for total war with the Soviet Union, he told his publisher Fred Warburg, "and the new weapons, of which of course the atomic bomb is the most powerful and most publicized." It lay also "in the acceptance of a totalitarian outlook by intellectuals of all colours," and the corruption of language that accompanied it.

This drift—and the threat it posed to civil liberties—provided the theme for Orwell's last and most famous novel, *Nineteen Eighty-Four* (1949); but the political, social, and economic conditions leading up to that situation had been his concern for a long time, as early as *Homage to Catalonia* (1939), about the Spanish Civil War, and *Animal Farm* 1945), the brilliant Swiftian fable that became a best seller and later a popular film.

Contrary to popular opinion, *Nineteen Eighty-Four* (1949) is not about Stalinist Russia or Hitler's Germany, but about Great Britain and countries with similar forms of government, including the United States. It is a warning about what could happen to a democratic nation that centers all its energy and resources on war-making, on "right thinking," and on repressing points of view that conflict with the status quo. The novel ends with two powerful images of totalitarianism, one of "a boot stamping on a human face — forever," and another of Winston Smith's loving Big Brother. In the last scene, Smith smiles at the telescreen, "two gin-scented tears trickling down the side of his nose."

Orwell's warning may sound absurd to us who have survived the "real" 1984; and several critics have suggested that his prophecy was off the mark. But anyone who has paid attention to American history since 1945 will recognize those moments when American politics approached this absurdity.

During the 1950s, for example, militant anti-communism flourished under the leadership of Senator Joseph McCarthy and—with the complicity of Republicans and Democrats who should have known better—polluted the atmosphere. In such an atmosphere, as Orwell pointed out, everyone loses, especially those people so blinded by hatred and prejudice that they no longer know the difference between imaginary ills and real ones.

Under later administrations, the Orwell condition periodically recurred. Ronald Reagan, for example, described the Soviet Union as an "evil empire," and administrative statements about Latin America and about a "winnable" nuclear war resembled Big Brother's diatribes on the telescreen in *Nineteen Eighty-Four*. When this language was accompanied by censorship of the press, during the invasion of Grenada, Americans of every political persuasion—conservative, liberal, or radical—began to feel that basic democratic rights were endangered. From Thomas Paine to George Orwell, "common sense" indicates that totalitarianism is best resisted not by labels, fear tactics, and belligerence, but by open and lively debate and freedom of information.

In *Nineteen Eighty-Four,* especially the epilogue on Newspeak, and in "Politics and the English Language," the most important essay on language in the 20th century, Orwell argued that cleaning up our language, making it more precise and concrete, improved our politics as well. He did this in his own writing through images—pictures and sensations—that left no doubt about the meaning of his argument. This was true when he focused on the injustices of his time or on the simple pleasures of everyday life: flowers in spring; strong, properly brewed tea; and the English countryside.

"Politics and the English Language," for example, which says that political language in our time "is designed to make lies sound truthful and murder respectable, and to give an appearance of solidity to pure wind," describes easily recognizable abuses of language from recent history.

> Defenseless villages are bombarded from the air, the inhabitants driven out into the countryside, the cattle machinegunned, the huts set on fire with incendiary bullets; this is called *pacification*. Millions of peasants are robbed of their farms and sent trudging along the roads with no more than they can carry; this is called *transfer of population* or *rectification of frontiers*.

"Such phraseology is needed," Orwell went on to say, "if one wants to name things without calling up mental pictures of them."

At a time when many of the ills that Orwell warned against still flourish, readers do well to return to the words and example of this just, rather witty, and very honest man. An unsparing critic of all undemocratic practices, he once described his reason for writing in this way: "Every line of serious work I have written since 1936 has been written directly and indirectly *against* totalitarianism and for democratic socialism." A writer of astonishing integrity, he held to that position, through years of neglect, poverty, and three final years of illness, while completing *Nineteen Eighty-Four*.

Born Eric Arthur Blair, in Motlhari, Bengal (Burma), on June 25, 1903, "George Orwell" moved back to England as a child with his mother just before his father retired from the Indian Civil Service. Orwell attended two prestigious schools on scholarship, St. Cyprian's, which he described in "Such, Such Were the Joys," and Eton. Rather than go on to the university, he joined the Imperial Indian Police in 1922, and served in various posts in Burma until 1927. Reconciled to becoming a writer, he spent much of the next two years in Paris in rather severe poverty, as a dishwasher, tutor, and teacher. This experience and two years living among tramps in England provided material for *Down and Out in Paris and London* (1933). Subsequently he taught "at one of the most godforsaken places I have ever struck," and worked in a bookshop, while he wrote two novels and an account of working-class life in England. After his marriage to Eileen O'Shaughnessy in 1936, he went to fight on the Republican side against Franco, in the Spanish Civil War. Wounded and ill from tuberculosis, he lived in Morocco for a year.

Physically unfit for service in the army during World War II, Orwell joined the Local Defense Volunteers, worked for the BBC, and wrote for a Socialist weekly as literary editor. The publication of *Animal Farm* in 1945, the year of his wife's death, made him famous on both sides of the Atlantic. No longer financially dependent on jobs as a journalist, he moved to the island of Jura, in Scotland; there, in declining health, he completed his last novel, *Nineteen Eighty-Four*. Returning to a sanitorium in England and, later, a hospital in London, he married Sonia Brownell in October 1949 and died three months later, on

January 21, 1950. He remains, thirty-five years later, the most essential writer of our time.

Orwell's best epitaph is in "Why I Write," about his wish to make political writing into an art:

> My starting point is always a feeling of partisanship, a sense of injustice. . . . But I could not do the work of writing a book, or even a long magazine article, if it were not also an aesthetic experience. . . . So long as I remain alive and well I shall continue to take pleasure in solid objects and scraps of useless information. It is no use trying to suppress that side of myself. The job is to reconcile my ingrained likes and dislikes with the essentially public, non-individual activities that this age forces on all of us.

By George Orwell

The Collected Essays, Journalism, and Letters of George Orwell, 4 vols. Edited by Sonia Orwell and Ian Angus. New York: Harcourt, Brace, and World, 1968.

Animal Farm. New York: Harcourt, Brace, 1954.

Homage to Catolonia. New York: Harcourt, Brace, and World, 1952.

Nineteen Eighty-Four, A Novel. New York: Harcourt, Brace, 1949.

Down and Out in Paris and London, New York: Harcourt, Brace, and World, 1933.

And others.

ABOUT GEORGE ORWELL

Crick, Bernard R. *George Orwell: A Life*. Boston: Little, Brown, 1980.

George Orwell: A Collection of Critical Essays. Edited by Raymond Williams. Englewood Cliffs, New Jersey: Prentice Hall, 1974.

Woodcock, George. *The Crystal Spirit: A Study of George Orwell*. Boston: Little, Brown, 1966.

The World of George Orwell. Edited by Miriam Gross. New York: Simon and Schuster, 1973.

MERIDEL LeSUEUR

1900-

MERIDEL LeSUEUR WROTE IN 1976,

> I was born at the beginning of the swiftest and bloodiest
> century at Murray, Iowa, in a white square puritan house
> in the corn belt, of two physically beautiful people who had
> come west through the Indian and the Lincoln country. . .

being preachers, abolitionists, agrarians, radical lawyers on the Lincoln, Illinois, circuit. Dissenters and democrats and radicals through five generations.

In the fall of 1981, one of the few remaining survivors of the first American Writers' Congress of the radical 30s, LeSueur returned to New York City to help initiate a writers' union opposing the Reagan administration; and in the spring of 1983, she joined Philip Berrigan and five hundred other people in civil disobedience at Minneapolis Honeywell, a nuclear weapons manufacturer. Her slogan for that bicentennial year, "Survival is a form of resistance," remains her motto into her mid-80s, in a long life of affirmation and protest.

A short story writer, Meridel LeSueur belongs to a tradition of Midwestern radicals, people of indomitable strength who love the land, but who have no illusions about the harshness of life on the plains or of the insularity of the region's inhabitants. In "Corn Village" (1930), one of her earliest and best stories, the narrator says,

> Like many Americans I will never recover from my sparse childhood in Kansas. The blackness, weight, and terror of childhood in mid-America strike deep into the stem of life. Like desert flowers we learned to crouch near the earth, fearful that we would die before the rains, cunning, waiting the season of good growth.

The argument of "Corn Village" responds to expatriate writers of the 1920s, LeSueur's contemporaries, who went to Europe in an attempt to escape "the emptiness and ghostliness of mid-America." Unlike them, she was determined to dig down below the surface violence of Midwestern culture "not going to Paris or Morocco or Venice, instead staying with you, bringing you to life. For your life is my life and your death is mine also."

Referring to the writings of a previous generation, Sherwood Anderson's *Winesburg, Ohio* (1917) and Sinclair Lewis' *Main Street* (1920), LeSueur criticized the limitations of their regional caricatures. Lewis "has portrayed their grimaces, a seeming reality, but still only their faces in a mirror," she said; "Anderson of course has apprehended them with love, but that too has left out a great deal.''

This determination to convey the stark realities of the plains gives Midwestern literature its peculiar strength, as in the powerful, even bleak stories of Willa Cather, and the tough-minded and insistently moral essays of Carol Bly.

Working out West during the early 1930s, LeSueur began as a writer by making notes about how women ''suffered, how we were destroyed, macerated, ground out—and my pockets were full of these notes to the world, this cry from the belly.'' In the stories that followed, she juxtaposed physical hunger and spiritual abundance, economic poverty and fertile landscapes conveying a positive sense of experience like that in the songs of Woody Guthrie, the wandering balladeer of the radical 30s. Read by some Easterners as indictments of the prairies, LeSueur's stories actually confront the barrenness of people in every section of the country, urban and agrarian—in struggles of mothers bringing up children, the meanderings of alienated intellectuals, and the defeat of laborers at Ludlow, Colorado, and at the Sacco and Vanzetti trial.

Born on February 22, 1900, Meridel Wharton later took the name of her step-father, Arthur LeSueur, a socialist mayor of Minot, North Dakota. In her early years, she lived also in Fort Scott, Kansas, while her mother headed the English department at People's College, a school founded by Eugene Victor Debs and Helen Keller. In the years prior to World War I, LeSueur studied acting at the Academy of Dramatic Arts in New York City, where she lived in one of Emma Goldman's anarchist communes in Greenwich Village. In 1927, she published her first story in the *Dial,* the famous literary magazine edited by Schofield Thayer and Marianne Moore, and the following year moved to Minnesota, where her two daughters were born.

During the 1930s, LeSueur continued to write stories for leading publications, including *New Masses, Yale Review,* and *Kenyon Review.* In the early 1940s, on a Rockefeller Fellowship, she wrote *North Star Country,* a poetic history of the Northwest. Blacklisted during the McCarthy era, she published in communist magazines, and wrote children's books and articles for women's magazines under a *nom de plume.* After living somewhat under a cloud as a writer, LeSueur came to prominence again about 1970, during the early days of the women's movement; through the republication of her stories and novels, a new book of poems and some early journals, she became widely known and, in the Upper Midwest, where she lives, something of a folk heroine.

In her personal example, as well as in her better writings, LeSueur is an embodiment of 20th century people's history, calling up a past that usually appears only in regional histories or exceptional personal memoirs. Through her, the anarchist and socialist ideals have a voice and a name. What in other "proletarian" literature was merely rhetorical, in her work becomes concrete. In "I was Marching," set in the Minneapolis truckers' strike of 1937, for example, a young woman learns the joy of cooperation and resistance, and in "Annunciation," also from *Salute to Spring,* another woman, hungry and pregnant, takes the blossom-pear tree outside her window as a promise of better days.

By background and experience, LeSueur was prepared to address justice issues not as a preacher, someone with the "right" opinions, but as an artist who could show with authority and beauty the harsh reality and quiet strength of workers' lives. She was aware not only of obvious weaknesses of the system, but also of the hidden strengths that suggested movement, new directions, and new beginnings. Her literary art resembles the photographic art of Dorothea Lange, whose "Migrant Mother" caught the persistence as well as discouragement of a family victimized by the Depression.

Speaking once of the loss and rediscovery of her work, she referred to herself, appropriately, as "Mrs. Lazarus." Like the people at the center of her stories—the people Ma Joad talks about in Steinbeck's *The Grapes of Wrath,* these stories survive.

BY MERIDEL LESUEUR

Harvest: Collected Stories. Boston: West End Press, 1977.

"The Ancient People and the Newly Come." *Growing Up in Minnesota: Ten Writers Remember Their Childhoods*. Edited by Chester G. Anderson. Minneapolis: University of Minnesota Press, 1976.

Salute to Spring. New York: International Publishers, 1940, 1977.

And others.

ABOUT MERIDEL LESUEUR

Schleuning, Neala. *America We Sang Without Knowing: The Life and Ideas of Meridel LeSueur*. Markato, Minnesota. Little Red Hen Press, 1983.

DOROTHY DAY

1897-1980

DOROTHY DAY IS A MODEL FOR OUR TIME FOR SEVERAL REASONS.
First, because she was peculiarly, deeply, and undeniably
American, and thus brought a very special character to her life
as a Christian. Although she loved Russian, French, British,
and Italian novelists—particularly Dostoevsky, George Bernanos,
Dickens, Qrwell, and Ignazio Silone—she was a child of the
American experience, and her religious commitment as well as

her vocation was bound up with this country. Her early family life, which was casually religious, her formal education in public schools and at the University of Illinois, as well as her admiration for William James's *Varieties of Religious Experience,* shaped her sensibility. She was a disciple of the American radical tradition, persistently anarchist and religious, from Thomas Paine to Martin Luther King, Jr. Her close association with *The Masses,* Mike Gold, and Ammon Hennacy—as well as her admiration for Eugene Victor Debs, Emma Goldman, and Elizabeth Gurley Flynn—was formative and enduring. Peter Maurin, a French peasant, was her teacher once she became a Catholic; but her temper was in the American grain.

Second, because she was a member of the laity. Unlike many religious figures held up for imitation to young people, she was not a cleric. She belonged to that group that emerged as a shaping force in the church at the time of the Second Vatican Council. As a 20th century heroine who faced the anxieties and challenges of a violent century, she was not so far removed from us as to appear foreign or aloof.

Third, because she failed, like most people, at many things—as a wife, in an early marriage, and perhaps as a parent. Although many of us see Dorothy Day as triumphant, as a success, one must acknowledge also her judgment of her life in *The Long Loneliness* (1952): "I feel that I have done nothing well. But I have done what I could." She often said that she took on certain responsibilities only because others (Peter Maurin, Ammon Hennacy, Karl Meyer) pushed them upon her. Although faithful and resilient, she never pretended to be all-knowing or all-powerful.

> Sometimes the only thing that keeps a woman going is the necessity of taking care of her young. She cannot sink into lethargy and despair because the young ones are dragging at her skirts, clamoring for something—food, clothing, shelter, occupation. She is carried outside herself.

Fourth, because she was a writer, the kind of writer that the language needs at this moment. She understood the power of everyday speech, and wrote in a manner that was understandable to everyone. Although she had a complex and demanding message to communicate, she fashioned a style that shunned pretention, artifice, or "rhetoric" in order to convey that message. On the works of mercy, she wrote, for example: "Martyrdom is not gallantly standing before a firing squad. Usually it is the losing of a job because of not taking a loyalty oath or buying a war bond, or paying a tax. Martyrdom is small, hidden, misunderstood." Elsewhere, in a meditation on the virtue of obedience, she said:

> Obedience is a matter of love, which makes it voluntary, not compelled by fear or force. Pope John's motto was "Obedience and Peace." Yet he was the pope who flouted conventions which had hardened into laws as to what a pope could and could not do, and the Pharisees were scandalized and the people delighted.

Fifth, because she internalized values associated with peace and justice and gave them substance. In her devotion to voluntary poverty, to nonviolence, and to the radical reconstruction of the social order, she lived among workers, radicals, prisoners, and the down and out. For Christians, she came as a great shock. Here, in the life and vocation of one woman were the values that had been held up to church members, but often by people who did not embody them. Through her, the words became flesh: devotion to the poor, resistance to war, vulnerability toward circumstance, and charity to everyone.

Born in Brooklyn, on November 8, 1897, Dorothy Day lived briefly in San Francisco, but grew up in Chicago, where her father worked as a journalist. At 15, she won a scholarship to the University of Illinois and there became a socialist. Two years later, she returned to New York City, where she lived most of her life. As a young radical, she was arrested with the Wobblies (Industrial Workers of the World) and the suffragettes, as she was later with war resisters and United Farm Workers. During World War I, she wrote for the *Masses* and during the 20s lived in Greenwich Village, where she became friends with Eugene O'Neill, Malcolm and Peggy Cowley, Allen Tate, Caroline Gordon, and Kenneth Burke. At that time, she worked as a nurse, wrote a novel, *The Eleventh Virgin,* married, and lived briefly in Mexico.

In 1926, Day's conversion to Catholicism led to her separation from her second husband, Foster Batterham, and to a break with some of her radical friends. During those years, she supported herself and her only daughter, Tamar Teresa, by writing for *America, Commonweal,* and other periodicals.

On May 1, 1933, five months after meeting Peter Maurin, Dorothy Day founded *The Catholic Worker,* a monthly newspaper dedicated to making known "the expressed and implied teachings of Christ." It is published today, as it was over fifty years ago, at a penny a copy, with a circulation of 100,000. In the years between 1933 and her death in December 1980, Dorothy Day lived at various Houses of Hospitality and Catholic Worker farms near New York City, edited the newspaper, wrote five books, and spoke frequently at colleges, universities, churches and Catholic Worker communities throughout the United States.

Over those decades, she emerged as the most remarkable person in the history of American Catholicism and in some ways the most influential. Although few people managed, like her, to make a total commitment to voluntary poverty, personalism, or Christian anarchism, they often learned a great deal from her, and some went on to significant vocations modeled on her example.

Through her work—feeding the poor and housing the homeless, through her newspaper and her monthly column, "On Pilgrimage," and through her war tax resistance and civil disobedience, Dorothy Day touched the lives of numerous people: workers, intellectuals, students, clergy, and women of three generations. Among the writers and editors who, at various times, helped to edit *Catholic Worker* are Michael Harrington, author of *The Other America;* John Cogley, James O'Gara, and John Cort, editors of *Commonweal*; Tom Cornell and James Forest, co-founders of the Catholic Peace Fellowship; James Cook, author of *Rags of Time: A Season and Prison:* as well as a host of other artists and radicals who contributed to its pages: Ammon Hennacy, W.H. Auden, Gordon Zahn, Ade Bethume, Thomas Merton, Daniel Berrigan, Philip Berrigan, Eileen Egan, Fritz Eichenberg, Rita Corbin.

When Dorothy Day died, December 1980, she was mourned by the down-and-out in Manhattan, whom she fed and clothed, as well as by the great and famous, including the cardinal archbishop of New York, who came to bless her coffin. Many regard her as a saint.

BY DOROTHY DAY

By Little and By Little: The Selected Writings of Dorothy Day. Edited by Robert Ellsberg. New York: Alfred A. Knopf, 1983.

The Dorothy Day Book: A Selection from Her Writings and Readings. Edited by Margaret Quigley and Michael Garvey. Springfield, Illinois: Templegate Press, 1982.

On Pilgrimage: The Sixties. New York: Curtis Books, 1972.

Loaves and Fishes. New York: Harper and Row, 1963. 1983.

The Long Loneliness: An Autobiography. New York: Harper and Row, 1952 (1982).

ABOUT DOROTHY DAY

Coles, Robert. *A Spectacle Unto the World: The Catholic Worker Movement.* Photographs by Jon Erikson. New York: Viking, 1973.

Miller, William D. *A Harsh and Dreadful Love: Dorothy Day and the Catholic Worker Movement.* New York: Liveright, 1973.

Piehl, Mel. *Breaking Bread: The Catholic Worker and the Origin of Catholic Radicalism in America.* Philadelphia: Temple University Press, 1982.

AMMON HENNACY

1894-1970

AMMON HENNACY WAS ARRESTED THIRTY-TWO TIMES DURING HIS lifetime for various acts of civil disobedience—in Omaha, in New York City, and in his native Ohio (during the First World War). From 1918 to 1922, he did time for draft resistance, in Atlanta Federal Prison, where Eugene Victor Debs and Alexander Berkman, Emma Goldman's lover, were confined about the same time.

After his release from that prison, Ammon and his common-law wife, Selma, walked across much of the United States and climbed Pike's Peak, in Colorado. That activity was a kind of therapy, Dorothy Day said, after the hard times in solitary confinement. Ammon had been so confined after leading a strike against conditions in the Atlanta jail when he learned that the guards dined on food meant for the inmates while serving the prisoners spoiled fish.

Ammon said that his moral education began with that imprisonment, although he had previously showed extraordinary courage in standing against conscription during World War I. One of the most moving passages in his autobiography, *The Book of Ammon* (1965), describes his time in solitary, his journey out of despair, and his gradual conversion to Christian nonviolence:

> I had passed through the idea of killing myself. This was an escape, not any solution to life. The remainder of my two years in solitary must result in a clear-cut plan whereby I could go forth and be a force in the world. . . .Gradually I came to gain a glimpse of what Jesus meant when he said that the Kingdom of God must be in everyone: in the deputy, the warden, in the rat, and the pervert. To change the world by bullets or ballots was a useless procedure. . . . Therefore the only revolution worthwhile was the one man revolution within the heart. Each one would make this by himself and not need to wait on a majority.

Born in Negley, Ohio, on July 24, 1893, Ammon Hennacy joined the Ohio Socialist Party and the Industrial Workers of the World (the Wobblies) at sixteen. After a year at Hiram College, he went to the University of Wisconsin, where he once gave up his bed to Randolph Bourne, the social and literary critic who had come to speak in Madison in 1914. From there Ammon returned to Ohio State University for a year and then to full-time organizing for the party of Eugene Victor Debs and for resistance to the draft. Following the prison term in Atlanta, he visited radical communes, farmed in Wisconsin, and wrote for various radical periodicals, including *Mother Earth,* founded earlier by Emma Goldman.

As a social worker in Milwaukee in the 1930s, he lived with his wife Selma and two daughters, Carmen and Sharon. After 1937, when he met Dorothy Day, he became a contributor to the *Catholic Worker*. Their first meeting, important to both of them, is described early on in his autobiography:

> Dorothy Day spoke at the Social Action Congress in Milwaukee, being invited there by Bishop (later Cardinal) Strich. . . . In answering questions from patriotic questioners she mentioned something of my pacifist record, saying that I was not a Catholic, but an anarchist and that when the next war came she would be with me in opposition to it. Her continued refusal to follow the party line of most churchmen in praising Franco gained my admiration.

The uncompromised principles and the practical wisdom, the idea and the deed, appear side by side in *The Book of Ammon*, as well as in his posthumously published *The One Man Revolution in America* (1970), a collection of portraits of and quotations from *his* eighteen great Americans, from John Woolman, Thomas Paine, and Thomas Jefferson (the only president in the group), to Dorothy Day and Malcolm X. As an anarchist Ammon would not allow his two books to be published commercially; that meant earning money for the tax collection and, therefore, for warmakers. These extraordinary works, privately printed, are now available from his widow (Joan Thomas, P.O. Box 25, Phoenix, Arizona 85001, $5.00 each, plus postage). Although casual in style and organization, they belong in every public library and peace education center.

Ammon Hennacy was, I think, the most courageous man I have ever known, in his insistence on speaking truth to power and in resisting injustice. Being with him or hearing him lecture—on a street corner, on a talk show, or in an auditorium, one felt as if he had suddenly caught the pulse of the American radical tradition. Even at 70, Ammon's face was animated and friendly, although lined from years spent laboring in the fields, on the picket line, and in prison.

It would be ridiculous, however, to romanticize Ammon Hennacy. He could be contentious, cantankerous, and stubborn, often confronting his listener with theories on nutrition (''no fish, flesh, or fowl'') or his favorite sayings on obscure subjects. He advised reading the morning newspaper ''to find out what the bastards are up to today.'' Persistent in his radicalism and repetitious in his teaching, he brought many people into movements for social change by selling *The Catholic Worker* on the street corner and by his own example. Dorothy Day, who said Ammon's books resembled Thoreau's, but with a sense of humor, admitted that he had challenged her into taking a stand on issues that she might otherwise have neglected.

In the 1960s, Ammon opened a Catholic Worker House for ex-prisoners and others on the road in Salt Lake City. It was named for Joe Hill, the Wobblie organizer and balladeer who was killed by the state of Utah in 1915. (Joan Baez and others sing the famous song immortalizing him: ''I dreamed I saw Joe Hill last night/ alive as he could be.'') Ammon took a grocery cart to nearby supermarkets each morning to beg food—day-old bread and vegetables for the soup line at his House of Hospitality. Each year, even while picketing daily against capital punishment, he fasted one day for each year since 1945 when the atomic bomb fell on Hiroshima and Nagasaki.

He was a crusty old Irishman with a marvelous capacity for talk and a love of poetry, especially William Blake and Edwin Markham. Many people, in fact, found him *too* gregarious. Like Peter Maurin, the co-founder of the Catholic Worker movement, Ammon never tired of preaching the gospel of Christian anarchism. Though critical of anyone who ''chickened out'' in the struggle for peace, he was also kind and generous, and able to appreciate the best in people who disagreed with him (and most people did).

Ammon's numerous actions in the nonviolent tradition included protests against capital punishment and against mock atomic-air-raid drills in Manhattan in the 1950s. His last leaflet, with the heading ''Thou Shalt Not Kill,'' was distributed on the picket line in front of the state capitol building in Salt Lake City shortly before he died of a heart attack in early January 1970. Among the many statements for which he is remembered is this bit of wisdom, written after a day in the fields, in 1945.

> Love without courage and wisdom is sentimentality, as
> with the ordinary church member. Courage without love
> and wisdom is foolhardiness, as with the ordinary soldier.
> Wisdom without love and courage is cowardice, as with
> the ordinary intellectual. Therefore one who has love,
> courage, and wisdom is one in a million, who moves the
> world, as with Jesus, Buddha, and Gandhi.

BY AMMON HENNACY

The One Man Revolution in America. Salt Lake City: Ammon Hennacy
Publications, 1970.

The Book of Ammon, originally published as *Autobiography of a Catholic
Anarchist.* New York: Catholic Worker Books, 1954.

ABOUT AMMON HENNACY

Day, Dorothy. "Picture of a Prophet." *Loaves and Fishes.* New York:
Harper and Row, 1963.

Piehl, Mel. *Breaking Bread: The Catholic Worker and the Origin of Catholic
Radicalism in America.* Philadelphia: Temple University Press, 1982.

WILFRED OWEN

1893-1918

EVERYONE, GANDHI SAID, MUST HAVE A TEXT TO EXAMINE, TO compare, and to test his or her life against. For this purpose, the writings of recent poets and artists have been especially valuable sources of inspiration and wisdom for people working in social justice. Since the Vietnam war this has been especially true for the writings of Wilfred Owens, a young poet who died in the

First World War, whose poems also provided the text for Benjamin Britten's moving oratorio, *War Requiem* (1963).

Among modern writers, no one understood and revealed the philosophical and religious implications of modern warfare better than Wilfred Owen, writing from the Western Front, 1916-18. In these letters and poems, he struggled with the basic conflict between his life as a soldier and the Christian commandment of love, between his everyday condition and the ethics of nonviolence.

In Owen's writings, "the language of the Bible rises like water in the well of his subconscious mind, polluted by war, like the ravaged countryside where he fought and died," his biographer, Jon Stallworthy, has said. Owen's letter to a friend in June 1918, for example, spoke in this way of having drilled his troops with helmets and rifles the day before:

> For 14 hours yesterday I was at work—teaching Christ to lift his cross by numbers, and how to adjust his crown; and not to imagine thirst till after the last halt. I attended his supper to see that there were no complaints, and inspected his feet to see that they would be worthy of the nails. I see to it that he is dumb and stands to attention before his accusers. With a piece of silver I buy him every day, and with maps I make him familiar with the topography of Golgotha.

The passage is a characteristic one, a statement, like so many of his poems, that is self-accusing without self-pity. In it, Owen indicates a sound awareness of how, as an officer in charge of troops, he could not extricate himself from the barbarous task of war. By his acts, he implicated himself as surely as Pilate's soldiers or Caesar's armies involved themselves in the death of Christ at Golgotha, "the place of the skull." Owen speaks not of hereditary or generalized guilt, but of his personal responsibility for actions on the side of death.

Wilfred Owen was, at the time of this letter to Osbert Sitwell, twenty-five years old. The oldest child of a lower middle-class family, he was born in Ostwestry, England, on March 18, 1893, and attended grammar schools in Birkenhead and

Shrewsbury, but did not qualify for a university scholarship. He educated himself, nonetheless, through courses at the university college in Reading, an hour west of London, and through work as a tutor in England and France before the war. Those years included time as a lay assistant at the vicarage of Reverend Herbert Wigan, in Dunsden. At nineteen, Owen thought seriously of becoming an Episcopal priest himself, but went through a religious crisis prompted by a disillusionment with conventional Christianity. About the same time, he rediscovered the poems of John Keats, and once in the army rapidly matured as a poet.

Wounded at the front, he returned to England in 1917 at Craiglockhart Hospital, near Edinburgh. There he met Siegfried Sassoon, a published poet, who encouraged him; eventually Owen published a few lyrics in leading periodicals, powerful poems suggesting an acutely modern sensibility, revolutionary for the time. By June 1918, he was back on the Western Front, in the north of France, and on November 4 of that year, one week before the Armistice, after successfully leading his troops across a canal near Ors, he was killed. Although Owen left only a small body of work, his posthumously collected poems are generally regarded as some of the masterworks of modern literature and, indeed, in the canon of English poetry.

A good example of this achievement is "Futility," written about the same time as the prose statement quoted above. The speaker in the poem is a soldier who stands above the body of his dead comrade, asking, in despair: "Was it for this the clay grew tall?" Dazed, the speaker wonders why the sun, that once brought life and stars out of the cold earth, is now powerless to raise his comrade from the dead?

Futility

Move him into the sun —
Gently its touch awoke him once,
At home, whispering of fields unsown.
Always it woke him, even in France.
Until this morning and this snow.
If anything might rouse him now
The kind old sun will know.

Think how it wakes the seeds,—
Woke, once, the clays of a cold star.
Are limbs, so dear achieved, are sides,
Full-nerved—still warm—too hard to stir?
Was it for this the clay grew tall?
—O what made fatuous sunbeams toil
To break earth's sleep at all?

The questions in the second stanza are posed to no one in particular, yet the implication remains that God, in a sense, is on trial. Why did He bother creating the earth if—in the end—a young man at the height of his powers, in strength, beauty, and intelligence, must die so meaninglessly? Why did He make the sun so powerful, if it cannot—in all its glory—raise this young man, the end point of a diverse and complicated evolutionary process, to life?

The questions posed by Owen's poems seem almost instinctive. How can anyone, particularly a religious person, he asks, stand casually by while the forces of death triumph all around? Such provocative questions with psychological and political as well as religious implications suggest at least two reasons for the continuing importance of his work: (1) Owen understood the significance of the First World War, in that it would profoundly alter the nature of religious belief, destroying the past or rendering it useless for many people. Human beings, in discovering the scale of destruction possible in mechanized warfare, were literally unhinged by that awareness, as Ernest Hemingway and T.S. Eliot would indicate in stories and poems of the 1920s; (2) Owen understood also how he, as an actor in history, was responsible for war's destruction, preparing his men, his other Christs, for the crown of thorns. He recognized that even with the best intentions, people capitulate to the forces of death, out of conformity, laziness, moral indifference.

Such cooperation with death eventually undermines not only a person's belief, but also the nature of the church, Owen said to his mother, in a 1917 letter.

Already I have comprehended a light which never will filter into the dogma of any national church; namely, one of

Christ's essential commands was. . . be bullied, be out-
raged, be killed; but do not kill. It may be chimerical and
an ignominious principle, but there it is. It can only be
ignored, and I think pulpit professionals are ignoring it very
skillfully.

In the same letter, Owen complained, "The practice of selective ignorance is one cause of war. Christians have deliberately
cut some of the main teachings of their code."

For Owen, the main teaching that had been cut was
Christ's disavowal of killing, and anyone trying to live as a Christian in this century is likely to be rather shocked by Owen's
pointed remark. In his poems, also, he gave a realistic view of
warfare, after the idealized view projected by the Romantic and
Victorian traditions. His antiwar sentiments, in fact, resembled
those of Leo Tolstoy's pamphlets on Christian tradition of nonviolence thirty years before. Coincidentally, during the early days
of the war, Owen lived in the home of a French poet influenced
by Tolstoy's writings, and sent home drawings of wounded
soldiers brought by train to the south of France.

Out of the depth of his imagination, Owen dramatized
the threat to life rendered by modern warfare. In ironic poems
such as "Dulce Et Decorum Est" and "Insensibility," he asked
conventional believers to recognize their failure to uphold the
teachings of Jesus and thereby focused attention on a major
dilemma for contemporary Christians.

Simone Weil's statement, during the Second World War,
that the distance separating the individual or the church from
the essential Christian message of peace results in a painful
spiritual state. In his poems and letters, Wilfred Owen arrived
at a similar truth thirty years before. It is one that must be
recognized, he thought, if the ethics of Christianity are ever to
inform people's lives and actions. This is especially true in an
age when everyone, as Owen said, lives on an extended battle-
field and where, in a nuclear age, "Christ dies daily in No Man's
Land."

BY WILFRED OWEN

Wilfred Owen: War Poems and Others. Edited by Dominic Hibberd. London: Chatto and Windus, 1975.

The Collected Poems of Wilfred Owen. Edited by C. Day Lewis. New York: New Directions, 1964, 1965.

ABOUT WILFRED OWEN

Hibberd, Dominic. *Wilfred Owen.* British Council Pamphlet. London: Longman Group Ltd., 1975.

Stallworthy, Jon. *Wilfred Owen: A Biography.* New York: Oxford University Press, 1974.

ELIZABETH GURLEY FLYNN

1890-1964

AMMON HENNACY, AMERICAN ANARCHIST AND CATHOLIC worker, admired people, as he said, "who never chickened." Among those whom he praised for her consistency and courage was Elizabeth Gurley Flynn, whose life was dedicated to gaining rights for and improving conditions of workers. With Eugene Victor Debs and Emma Goldman, Flynn is one of the great radicals of the early 20th century, who suffered for her persistence: loss of her husband and a lover, dismissal from the civil liberties organization she co-founded, and—at sixty—imprisonment.

As a young woman Flynn, like Abby Kelley Foster, was famous for her beauty; with her clear voice and golden-red hair, she was a striking presence on the lecture platform and the picket line. In a memoir at the time of Flynn's death, Dorothy Day recalled the young rebel's effect on a crowd:

> She charmed us out of our meager money; people emptied their pockets when the collection was taken for the strikers. I forsook all prudence and emptied my purse, not even leaving myself carfare to get back to the office. . . .In this way she aided countless workers—miners through the far West, workers in wheat, lumber, textiles, all have benefited from her early work.

Flynn gave her first speech for socialism at 16, in 1906, in the Bronx, with the encouragement of her parents and to the delight of reporters for the New York newspapers. From then until her death at seventy-four, she was the subject of articles detailing her defense of Wobblies in the Pacific Northwest and the Mesabi Iron Range; her stormy love affair with Carlo Tresca, the hero of the Lawrence, Massachusetts, strike in 1912; and other labor and civil liberties disputes. To her many other causes she added, during her last years, that of prison reform; and *My Life as a Political Prisoner* (1963), about her twenty-eight months in Alderson (W. Va.) Federal Reformatory, is a powerful indictment of the system.

Born in Concord, New Hampshire, on August 7, 1890, Elizabeth Gurley Flynn grew up in the Bronx, where her mother insisted they settle in 1900. Her father, a ne'er-do-well, whom Elizabeth later accused of hiding behind her ''radicalism'' as an excuse for not holding a job, encouraged her interest in socialism. She read widely in the utopian novels and tracts of Mary Wollstonecraft, Edward Bellamy, and William Morris, and in her youth admired the anarchists Emma Goldman and Alexander Berkman, whom she met and followed. She joined the Industrial Workers of the World during its first year, in 1906, and two years later married John Archibald Jones, a miner active in the I.W.W. She had two sons by Jones, one of whom died in infancy; the second, reared principally by Elizabeth's mother and sister, died in 1940. After divorcing Jones, who expected her to give up organizing and agitation, Elizabeth Gurley fell in love with Carlo Tresca, a handsome Italian anarchist. Although they separated about 1930, she mourned him for many years after his death in 1943.

Victimized by various laws harassing radicals, particularly during the Red Scare following World War I, Flynn combined labor organizing and legal defense for workers. From 1926 to 1930, she chaired the International Labor Defense, many of whose members were affiliated with the Communist party; in 1930, she herself joined the party. In 1940, the American Civil Liberties Union, which she had helped to establish, expelled her from its executive board because of her communist affiliations, a decision rescinded only after her death.

In the second Red Scare, after World War II, Flynn was indicted for advocating the overthrow of the United States government. Later she described a typical political arrest in the McCarthy days:

> On a hot morning in June, 1951, the bell of our apartment on East 12th Street in New York City rang insistently. A knock came on the door, too soon for anyone to have climbed the three flights of stairs after we had pressed the button to open the downstairs door.
>
> Three F.B.I. agents, two men and a woman, roughly pushed their way past [my sister]. They stated they had a warrant for my arrest. I took the document and read it. It was for alleged violation of the infamous Smith Act. "For teaching and advocating the violent overthrow of the government, when and if circumstances permit," it said.

With several of her old associates, some crippled with age, one routed from a nursing home, she was brought to prison, where she endured further humiliation.

The second step after entering was to strip and leave all one's clothes in a side room where they were searched by an officer, while the prisoner was wrapped in a sheet and taken to the showers. Next we were ordered to take an enema and to climb on an examination table for examination. All openings of the body were roughly searched for narcotics by "a doctor"—a large woman who made insulting remarks about Communists who did not appreciate this country. I told her to mind her business. Once she became so animated in her opinions while she was taking a blood specimen that she allowed the blood to run down my arm. "Watch what you are doing," I said. "Never mind my politics, watch my blood."

Refusing to cooperate with the government in naming her associates in the party, she was sentenced to the federal penitentiary, where she remained from January 1955 to May 1957. A famous case involving her and the Marxist historian Herbert Aptheker brought a legal victory before the Supreme Court and enabled her to travel abroad. In the early 1960s, she visited several times in the Soviet Union. When she died in Moscow, on September 5, 1964, she received a state funeral in Red Square.

In a long, eventful, and often stormy public life, Flynn participated in most of the major struggles for justice during the first half of this century. Her autobiography, *The Rebel Girl* (1976), gives a detailed and instructive account of the education of a woman whose life was lived for the benefit of others. She gave up easier and more conventional careers in order to side with the workers, a choice that Dorothy Day suggested had religious implications.

Gurley Flynn was of the laity, and she was also my sister in the deep sense of the word. She always did what the laity is nowadays urged to do. She felt a responsibility to do all in her power in defense of the poor, to protect them against injustice and destitution.

The title of Flynn's autobiography is taken from a song written for her by Joe Hill, the Swedish immigrant laborer and

Wobblie balladeer. She had come to Hill's defense when he was arrested and brought to trial, as she had for so many young radicals; and Hill's words, later set to a ragtime tune, are a fitting tribute to "the rebel girl":

> There are women of many descriptions
> In this queer world as everyone knows.
> Some are living in beautiful mansions,
> And wearing the finest of clothes.
> There are blue-blooded queens and princesses,
> All dressed in diamond and pearl.
> But the only and thoroughbred lady
> Is the rebel girl.

BY ELIZABETH GURLEY FLYNN

The Alderson Story: My Life as a Political Prisoner. New York: International Publishers, 1963.

The Rebel Girl: An Autobiography—My First Life (1906-1926). New York: International Publishers, (1955) 1973.

ABOUT ELIZABETH GURLEY FLYNN

Camp, Helen C. "Flynn." *Notable American Women: The Modern Period: A Biographical Dictionary.* Edited by Barbara Sicherman and Carol Hard Green. Cambridge, Mass.: Harvard University Press, 1980.

Day, Dorothy. "Elizabeth Gurley Flynn." *By Little and by Little: Selected Writings by Dorothy Day.* Edited by Robert Ellsberg. New York: Alfred A. Knopf, 1983.

RANDOLPH BOURNE
1886-1918

IN THE 1920S AND 30S, MANY WRITERS AND INTELLECTUALS REMEM-
bered the First World War as a tragic, even pointless error; but
during the four long years of the "senseless slaughter," as Ernest
Hemingway called it, few of them publicly opposed the war. Bertrand Russell, who lost his Cambridge University fellowship and
went to prison because of war resistance, was a dissenter; so was

Randolph Bourne, who endured harassment and neglect because of his public opposition to American intervention. The theme of his essays, critical of Woodrow Wilson and the war fever, was summarized in an ironic phrase, "War is the health of the State."

In the postwar decade, Bourne was a guiding spirit for young writers and artists in Greenwich Village and influenced the "new" *Dial* magazine, 1920-29, edited by an admirer Schofield Thayer. Since then, such diverse social critics as Theodore Dreiser and John Dos Passos, Edward Dahlberg and Noam Chomsky have regarded Bourne as a model of honesty and personal courage and as an intellectual hero of this century.

Born in Bloomfield, New Jersey, on May 30, 1886, Randolph Bourne was physically disfigured at birth and progressively deformed later by spinal tuberculosis, but this deformity seldom impeded his vigorous, multi-faceted early career. After high school, where he indicated a talent for writing and a keen interest in the social sciences, he worked in factories and offices in New Jersey and New York City for four years before entering Columbia University on scholarship in 1909. Harsh conditions among workers and the precariousness of their lives shaped the sensibility of the young writer and prompted his commitment to socialism during his undergraduate years.

In 1913, an article on youth in *Atlantic Monthly* brought Bourne to the attention of editors and readers; that summer, he completed an M.A. degree at Columbia and left on a traveling fellowship to Europe. He returned from there on the eve of the war, having witnessed the chaos that led to "the guns of August," 1914. For the next three years he worked hard, but unsuccessfully, to keep America neutral; and his essays between April 1917 and the armistice in 1918 charted the effects of the war fever on the youthful spirit of the times, and prophesied the disillusionment that was to characterize the post-war period. He died during the flu epidemic of December 1918 at 33 years of age.

"Call this thing that goes on in the modern schoolroom schooling, if you like. Only don't call it education." This was the first of several "disagreeable truths" that Bourne preached to his readers, in this case from the pages of the first issue of the *New Republic* magazine, November 7, 1914; over the next four years, until his premature death, he applied his vigorous intelligence to American politics and culture in a manner that was both original and prophetic. In the pages of the "old" *Dial* and the *Seven Arts,* he stood almost alone in condemning America's entry into World War I. In essays on education and the State, on the "new" poetry, fiction, and film, he also left a unique record of one man's struggle against intellectual conformity and the war-making state.

An admirer of William James and a student of John Dewey, Bourne brought a wide range of interests and experience to his discussion of "trans-national America," a country shaped by the immigrant migrations of the late 19th and early 20th centuries. His reflections on the promises and perils of the American experience focused on institutions such as the schools and the university, as well as on the arts—the poetry of Vachel Lindsay and Amy Lowell, the fiction of Willa Cather and Theodore Dreiser, the art of the cinema. He embraced early Modernism as an appropriate response to the new century and as a corrective to the cold intellectualism of the 19th century social engineers.

For Bourne the new pragmatism, in the writings of John Dewey, who supported the war, simply revived the old hazards of Puritanism, with its insensitivity to feeling and its self-righteousness. Such forces, masked as modern liberalism, squandered America's emotional capital, Bourne said, and perpetuated old errors. In sinning against the spirit of American promise, the social philosophers guided the nation "through sheer force of ideas into what the other nations entered only through predatory craft or popular hysteria or militarist madness." For Bourne, America's active participation on the side of Great Britain and France ended any chance of its providing any balance in an unstable world.

Bourne opposed the war not as an isolationist or idealist, but as an enlightened realist, since America's military involvement prevented it from serving as an arbiter between the Allies and the Central Powers. In "Below the Battle," he described a young man victimized by the intellectual and social forces of a nation at war. Though not afraid to die for his country, the youth obviously had no hatred of the enemy, Bourne argued, "even when the government decided that such animus is necessary to carry out its theories of democracy and the future organization of the world.'' Conscripted to fight, the draftee will go, but in the work of annihilation his youthful skepticism will turn to bitterness, Bourne said. And so it did.

In the midst of the war, Bourne came to understand the excesses of the modern state and the consequences for peacetime, especially the usurpation of the individual conscience by institutions established during times of stress. Under such tyranny, he argued, the desire for personal freedom becomes the impersonal instinct of the herd for conformity, creating a "conscience" no longer capable of distinguishing between good and evil, but only between what is acceptable to the state and what is unacceptable. His theme was to recur in numerous works later in the century, in such diverse writings as George Orwell's *Nineteen Eighty-Four,* Albert Camus's *The Rebel,* and Gordon Zahn's *German Catholics and Hitler's Wars.* In the Red Scare of 1919, when American radicals and labor agitators were imprisoned and exiled, Bourne's worst fears were confirmed.

In writing about cultural issues, Bourne drew upon his knowledge in many areas, the philosophy of education, adolescent psychology, political theory, and literary criticism. His artistic sensibility, attentive to the new directions in music and poetry, as well as fiction and film, enabled him to absorb the full impact of the war, when many of his contemporaries ignored its aesthetic and moral implications.

Bourne's portraits of young conscripts in his essays, for example, strongly resemble the fictional characters in the novels of the "lost generation" shortly afterward. And there are close similarities between the conscripts described in his anti-war essays and the three young Americans in John Dos Passos's novel *Three Soldiers* (1921), Frederick Henry in Ernest Hemingway's *A Farewell to Arms* (1929), and the disillusioned and psychologically troubled narrator of Robert Graves's memoir, *Goodbye to All That* (1929). Though older by several years, Bourne spoke a language similar to that of the soldiers in Wilfred Owen's ironic poems, "Futility" and "Dulce et Decorum Est Pro Patria Mori" (It is sweet and just to die for one's country).

In his honesty, "his relying on analysis rather than on rationalizations or ideologies,'' as Olaf Hansen has said, Bourne focused his attention on immediate experience rather than on abstract concepts or preconceived ideas. He treated culture and society as something lived rather than as something passively accepted.

A posthumously published "The History of a Literary Radical" described the intellectual tradition, from Thomas Paine to William James, that sustained Bourne in his social criticism. He called it "the new classicism," combining literary art and social thought, which he thought held promise for the future:

> Finding little in the American tradition that is not tainted with sweetness and light and burdened with the terrible patronage of bourgeois society, the new classicist will yet rescue Thoreau and Whitman and Mark Twain and try to tap through time a certain eternal human tradition of abounding vitality and moral freedom and so build out the future.

Bourne, a model for later social critics, redeemed the times by appreciating what the times made available, while refusing to be their prisoner.

BY RANDOLPH BOURNE

The Radical Will: Randolph Bourne Selected Writings, 1911-1918. Edited by Olaf Hansen. New York: Urizen Books, 1977.

War and Intellectuals: Collected Essays, 1915-1919. Edited by Carl Resek. New York: Harper and Row, 1964.

ABOUT RANDOLPH BOURNE

Moreau, John Adams. *Randolph Bourne: Legend and Reality.* Washington, D.C.: Public Affairs Press, 1966.

Schlissel, Lillian. *The World of Randolph Bourne.* New York: E.P. Dutton and Co., 1965.

BERTRAND RUSSELL

1872-1970

RECOGNIZING BERTRAND RUSSELL AS A GREAT MORAL LEADER OF this century is somewhat complicated by the fact that he was also one of its famous scoundrels. A characteristic remark in this vein was his comment to a woman friend in 1947: "How right you are about chastity. I gave it a good try once, but never again." An appropriate response from another woman friend was that if Russell thought that he was the nearest man could get to being God, he was close to being Satan as well.

Russell's refusal to endorse the war fever during World War I was, nonetheless, a courageous assault on the moral indifference of that period. For his pacifism, he lost a major fellowship at Cambridge University; from then until his death in 1970, at ninety-eight, he effectively exposed the immorality of pompous and pious Christians. While they went off to war, killing their brothers and sisters on the other side with easy consciences, Russell, the agnostic, withheld his approval and suffered the consequences of his dissent. With impressive logic and enviable humor, he won a permanent place in the history of movements for social justice, calling nations and their leaders to task for their inhumanity to one another and fostering a moral regeneration on issues of war and peace during the dark ages following World War II.

Although hesitant at times about supporting widespread civil disobedience, he was nonetheless an advocate of direct action, arguing in *Which Way to Peace?* (1936) that

> all great advances have involved illegality. The early Christians broke the law; Galileo broke the law; the French revolutionaries broke the law; early trade unionists broke the law. The instances are so numerous and so important that no one can maintain as an absolute principle obedience to constituted authority.

Or, as he said at the time of World War I: "I don't know how one *can* advocate an unpopular cause unless one is either irritating or ineffective."

Born in Revenscrot, Monmouthsire, England, on May 18, 1872, Bertrand Russell was reared by his grandmother, Lady Russell, wife of the former prime minister under Queen Victoria. His parents had both died by the time he was four. His brother Frank gave "Bertie" his first lessons in Euclid, which thrilled him and led to his early love of mathematics. After private tutoring, he entered Trinity College, Cambridge University in 1890, and was elected a fellow there five years later. The following year he married an American woman, Alys Smith, the first of four marriages, and traveled to the United States.

Elected a Fellow of the Royal Society in 1908, Russell collaborated with Alfred North Whitehead on *Principia Mathematica* (1910), and continued to lecture widely in Europe. Support for a conscientious objector and agitation against England's entrance into World War I got him into trouble. He lost his fellowship in 1916, and for writing against the war he later served six months in Brixton Prison, where he wrote *Introduction to Mathematical Philosophy*. The attitude that overtook him, as news about the slaughter on the Western Front poured in, surprised him.

> I have at times been paralyzed by skepticism, at times I have been cynical, at other times indifferent, but when the war came I felt as if I heard the voice of God. I knew that it was my business to protest, however futile protest might be. . . .As a lover of truth, the national propaganda of all the belligerent nations sickened me. As a lover of civilization, the return to barbarism appalled me. As a man of thwarted parental feeling, the massacre of the young wrung my heart.

In the early 20s, Russell traveled to Russia, China, and Japan, and ran for parliament as a member of the Labor Party. After a second marriage and parenthood, he returned to lecture several times in the United States, and in 1931, on the death of his brother, he became the Third Earl Russell, though he rarely used his title. In 1940, he gave the William James lectures at Harvard, an inquiry into meaning and truth, and then was refused permission to teach at the College of the City of New York because of his political and moral views. Re-elected to a fellowship at Trinity College, Cambridge, he continued to lecture widely both in his native country and abroad. In 1949, he was awarded the Order of Merit by the British government; and in 1950, he received the Nobel Prize for Literature, "in recognition of his many-sided and important work in which he constantly stood forth as a champion of humanity and freedom of thought."

Internationally famous at 30, Russell was destined for

immortality from the beginning, and the books by and about him are legion. His friends, associates, and students included many famous people of his time: Aldous Huxley, T.S. Eliot, Ludwig Wittgenstein, D.H. Lawrence, John Maynard Keynes. Sometimes regarded as the greatest logician since Aristotle, he combined a skeptical turn of mind with wicked wit and regarded "impersonal non-human truth as a delusion." A rationalist even in his eighties, he thought neither misery nor folly had any part in the inevitable lot of man. "And I am convinced that intelligence, patience, and eloquence can, sooner or later, lead the human race out of its self-imposed torture provided it does not exterminate itself meanwhile."

But the quality which gives Russell special claim on one's attention is his persistence in the pursuit of peace and justice. "Seldom indeed," wrote Daniel O'Connor, "has a philosopher shown such a sense of responsibility."

Faithfulness in upholding values of social justice has, of course, characterized the lives of many heroes of nonviolence. One thinks of Dorothy Day, at 78, arrested in California in support of the United Farm Workers; Ammon Hennacy, at 76, picketing the capitol building in Salt Lake City against capital punishment; and Eugene Victor Debs, at 65, serving a three-year sentence in Atlanta federal prison for draft resistance. Among those who persisted, however, Bertrand Russell, Nobel laureate and lord of the realm, may hold the record. Jailed at 89 for planning a demonstration advocating unilateral disarmament, he said later, "What I want is some assurance before I die that the human race will be allowed to continue." There were, at the same time, his speeches at rallies in Trafalgar Square against apartheid and against nuclear weapons, and the initiation of the Campaign for Nuclear Disarmament, which continues to thrive, more active than ever, in England and other European countries.

BY BERTRAND RUSSELL

The Autobiography of Bertrand Russell, 3 vols. New York: Allen Unwin, 1967, 1968, 1969.

The Basic Writings of Bertrand Russell. Edited by Robert E. Egner and Lester E. Dennon. New York: Simon and Schuster, 1961.

Why I Am Not a Christian and Other Essays on Religion and Related Subjects. New York: Simon and Schuster, 1957.

Portraits from Memory and Other Essays. New York: Simon and Schuster, 1956.

And many others.

ABOUT BERTRAND RUSSELL

Clark, Ronald W. *The Life of Bertrand Russell.* New York: Alfred A. Knopf, 1976.

MOHANDAS GANDHI

1869-1948

"THIS IS THE MAN," ROMAIN ROLLAND SAID OF GANDHI IN 1924, "who has stirred three hundred million people to revolt, who has shaken the foundations of the British Empire, and who has introduced into human politics the strongest religious impetus of the last two hundred years." But the most unusual tribute to Gandhi is undoubtedly George Orwell's, shortly before his death in 1950. Suspicious of pacifists and vegetarians, Orwell had to overcome most of his instincts to find anything good in a person venerated by so many: "Saints," his "Reflections on Gandhi" begins, "should always be judged guilty until they are proved innocent, but the tests that have to be applied to them are not, of course, the same in all cases."

After putting Gandhi to the test, Orwell comes down clearly on the side of the Mahatma ("great soul"), with a comment on his ability to "disinfect" the political air, as India and Great Britain settled down to decent and friendly relations. "One may feel, as I do, a sort of aesthetic distaste for Gandhi," Orwell said, and regard his basic aims "as anti-human and reactionary; but regarded simply as a politician, and compared with other leading political figures of our time, how clean a smell he has managed to leave behind!"

This rather minimalist endorsement of one of the great teachers of nonviolence is instructive, since it dramatizes the conflicting attitudes aroused by even the most consistent pacifist. It suggests as well how little is known and understood still about nonviolent approaches to social change.

In a relatively brief history, nonviolence made a great leap forward, nonetheless, during and through Gandhi's experiments with truth, and his writings, as well as the scholarship about him, provide the most extensive record available of its history. Among the items central to students are the film of Richard Attenborough, *Gandhi* (1982) and the psychoanalytic study, *Gandhi's Truth,* by Erik Erikson.

Mohandas Karamhand Gandhi was born on October 2, 1869, in Porbandar, India, on the Kathiawar peninsula, where his father was prime minister of the region. Married, according to custom, at thirteen, Gandhi attended Samaldas College, after completing the local high school. In 1888, leaving his wife and child, he sailed for England, where he was admitted to the Inner Temple to learn the law. Completing his studies and called to the bar in 1891, he returned to India, still rather infatuated with English tradition and finery.

Unsuccessful in his practice at home, Gandhi sailed for South Africa as an adviser to a Muslim in 1893. There he became active as an organizer in various associations and served in the ambulance corps during the Boer War. In 1903, after two years in India and the birth of his fourth son, he returned with his family to South Africa. Taking a vow of chastity at this time, he became more deeply involved, through his law practice in Johannesburg, in seeking a redress of grievances for Asians in South Africa. By this time he knew the essays of John Ruskin and Thoreau's *Civil Disobedience;* he also translated Tolstoy's *Letter to a Hindu* and established Tolstoy Farm, for Indian resisters. Imprisoned on several occasions, Gandhi was nonetheless successful in campaigns against discrimination, and by the time he returned to India in 1914, he was well-known in his home country. In 1909 he had written, while in jail, that one of the inner struggles of his life was "to bring Hindus and Muslims together."

In 1915, Gandhi founded his own ashram, a retreat for communal living, near Ahmedabad, in northern India, and began a campaign on behalf of millworkers. That continued, with mass civil disobedience, through the 1920s. His goal by this time was Indian independence from Great Britain, as well as peaceful co-existence between Hindus and Muslims. In prison, he wrote *Satyagraha* in South Africa, published essays in numerous periodicals, and read daily in the *Bhagavad Gita.*

In the early 1930s, following the proclamation of the Indian Declaration of Independence, Gandhi was imprisoned on several occasions, and in 1932, he announced a fast unto death in protest against the treatment of untouchables. His efforts for independence, which included a successful trip to England, continued through the early years of the Second World War. The struggle led to his and his wife's imprisonment, where they remained until her death in February 1944, and his release the following May. In 1947, he initiated another fast to bring an end to religious strife in India. A year later, on January 30, 1948, he was assassinated by a radical Hindu, as he moved through a crowd at Birla House, in New Delhi.

"We must widen the prison gates, and we must enter them as a bridegroom enters the bride's chamber. Freedom is to be wooed only inside prison walls and sometimes on gallows, never in council chambers, courts, or in the schoolroom," Gandhi wrote. The extent of his influence as a thinker is suggested by the frequency with which such statements serve as a source of inspiration and guidance for resisters throughout the world. This particular one provided the title for Philip Berrigan's fourth book, *Widen the Prison Gates,* written during his own imprisonment between 1970 and 1972. For almost every civil disobedient for justice in the latter 20th century, Gandhi, that "seditious Middle Temple lawyer and half-naked fakir," as Winston Churchill called him, has been a presence, a person to be contended with, either challenged or imitated.

Martin Luther King, Jr., in a famous photograph from the Civil Rights movement, is seated beneath a picture of Gandhi, and Daniel Berrigan, S.J., recorded his own reflections during his time in Danbury Federal, in *Lights on in the House of the Dead.* Numerous Americans have gone to India to learn how to appropriate Gandhi's spirit and tactics to later struggles for justice. Most recently, the Reverend Carl Kline, who initiated the peace witness of citizens from the United States on the borders of Nicaragua and Honduras, conducted such a pilgrimage as an apostle of Satyagraha (truth-seeking).

In this most violent of centuries, Gandhi's influence still manages, as Orwell said, to "disinfect" the political air; and Martin Luther King, Jr., Gandhi's principal American disciple, regarded his approach to social change as the only practical one for a nuclear age. "The choice," as King said, "is clearly between nonviolence and nonexistence."

By Mohandas Gandhi

An Autobiography: The Story of My Experiments with Truth. Boston: Beacon Press, 1962.

ABOUT MOHANDAS GANDHI

Erikson, Erik H. *Gandhi's Truth: On the Origins of Militant Nonviolence.* New York: W.W. Norton and Co., 1969.

Fischer, Louis. *Gandhi: His Life and Message for the World.* New York: New American Library, 1954.

Payne, Robert. *The Life and Death of Mahatma Gandhi.* New York: E.P. Dutton and Company, 1969.

EUGENE VICTOR DEBS

1855-1926

IN HIS EXCELLENT SOCIAL BIOGRAPHY OF DEBS, NICK SALVATORE
states a fact that should be kept in mind in remembering almost
every American radical, from Thomas Paine to Dorothy Day
and David Dellinger. Too often, Salvatore warns, Debs is regarded as a "larger-than-life hero," as someone born eternally at
odds with the culture around him. Such a view does violence

to Debs' full story, especially to the indigenous nature of his radicalism, nurtured as it was by the land, people, and traditions shared by most Americans.

Debs was a product of the American experience and his hope in the reconstruction of the social order resembled that of settlers from the 17th century to the present. At twenty-eight, for example, still under the influence of William Riley McKeen, whom Debs called "the model railroad president," he gave this ringing endorsement of America as "preeminently the land of great possibilities, of great opportunities, and of no less great probabilities. . . .We all have a fair chance and an open field. Long may it so remain. The time, the occasion is auspicious. Nothing like it was ever known before."

Such a statement is as representative of the man as his later and more famous statement at his sentencing for draft resistance in 1918: "While there is a lower class, I am in it; while there is a criminal element, I am of it; and while there is a soul in prison, I am not free." Five times the Socialist party's nominee for president of the United States, Debs received a significant percent of the vote on two occasions. Warren G. Harding, elected president in 1920, released Debs from Atlanta prison; earlier Woodrow Wilson had granted amnesty to other political prisoners after the war ended in 1918, but not to the popular Debs.

Ammon Hennacy, in Atlanta prison for draft resistance at about the same time, regarded Debs and Malcolm X as the two greatest Americans who ever lived. Hennacy admired Debs for his courage, but also for his faithfulness to the poor and the down-and-out. Debs' dedication to the railroad workers and the Wobblies did not end once he became a popular leader. He was not running for office or seeking a power base from which to launch a political career; he was a leader who cast his lot with workers and who remained loyal to them to the end.

Born on November 5, 1855, in Terre Haute, Indiana, where his parents had settled several years after immigrating from Alsace-Lorraine, Debs left school at fifteen to work on the railroad. Within five years he was secretary of the local Brotherhood of Locomotive Firemen. In 1885, the year of his marriage to Katherine Metzel, he was elected to the Indiana legislature as a Democrat, where he voted for measures that would now be regarded as anti-union.

In 1893, Debs helped to form the American Railway Union and subsequently became its president. The next year, when employees of the Pullman Company went out on strike, he took charge of the campaign, after some initial reservations, and later served a six-month prison sentence in the McHenry County (Ill.) jail for refusing to abide by a court injunction against the strikers.

In jail, a reading of Marx and Engels further radicalized Debs, and within four years, he was nominated for president by the Socialists. Shortly afterward, he became an editor of the party's weekly, *Appeal to Reason,* which eventually achieved a circulation of over 800,000. In the summer of 1905, in Chicago, Debs co-founded the Industrial Workers of the World, with Mother Jones, Lucy Parsons, and Big Bill Haywood; and although he later disagreed with the Wobblies, he always supported their right to organize. During the presidential campaign of 1908, Debs drew large crowds speaking from a train known as the "Red Special," and in the election of 1912, he polled almost a million votes, a figure exceeded in the election of 1920, when he campaigned from prison.

Debs' arrest in Canton, Ohio, in 1918, at a Socialist state convention, followed several warnings about his speaking against wartime conscription; but he believed strongly in the party's policy and its slogan, "Don't be a soldier, be a man." Sentenced to ten years for violation of the Espionage Act, he was one of many victims of the so-called Red Scare, during that repressive era in American history. (The actions of the Attorney General and an ambitious young lawyer named J. Edgar Hoover led to the deportation of Emma Goldman and two hundred and forty "radicals" in 1919 and the harassment and denial of basic civil liberties to many others.)

Although he remained active to the end, the time in prison weakened Debs' health. Back in Terre Haute, he wrote articles on prison conditions, published later as *Walls and Bars,* and continued leadership of the Socialist party. When he died in October 1926, 10,000 people attended the funeral services, and his home in Terre Haute is now a memorial to a man admired and loved by many. In 1971, when she received the annual Debs award, Dorothy Day spoke at his gravesite, acknowledging his influence on her own life, as a friend of the poor and as a writer and worker for social justice.

Among Debs' contributions to social history, as Nick Salvatore points out, were his understanding of the complex character of the democratic tradition and his ability to re-define it for the twentieth century. Integrating social and economic themes in a way that his audience understood, Debs recognized the central place of the class struggle and of social protest in American history, without ignoring cultural and religious traditions. "Christ," Debs argued, "organized a working class movement. . . for no other purpose than to destroy class rule and set up the common people as the sole and rightful inheritors of the earth." In this and similar statements, Debs showed his mastery of the political and religious exhortation characteristic of American oratory since the time of the Puritans. In his personal example, as well as in his national leadership, he is, as Salvatore says, "a constant reminder of the profound potential that yet lives in our society and in ourselves."

BY EUGENE VICTOR DEBS

Debs. Edited by Ronald Radosh. Englewood Cliffs, New Jersey: Prentice Hall, 1971.

Eugene V. Debs Speaks. Edited by Gene Y. Tussey. New York: Pathfinder Press, 1970.

Walls and Bars. Chicago: C.H. Kerr, (1927), 1973.

ABOUT EUGENE VICTOR DEBS

Ginger, Ray. *The Bending Cross: A Biography of Eugene Victor Debs.* New Brunswick, New Jersey: Rutgers University Press, 1949 (1962).

Salvatore, Nick. *Eugene V. Debs: Citizen and Socialist.* Urbana, IL: University of Illinois Press, 1982.

LEO TOLSTOY

1828-1910

IN THE HISTORY OF NONVIOLENCE, TOLSTOY AND GANDHI OCCUPY special places; among Americans, only Dorothy Day and Martin Luther King, Jr. enjoy such distinction. It was Tolstoy who confirmed the reputations of several American theoretians: William Lloyd Garrison, Henry David Thoreau, and Adin Ballou, whose writings Tolstoy cited after his own conversion to ''non-resistance,'' as he called it, in 1880. From then until his death in 1910, he wrote numerous letters, essays, and pamphlets that constitute a major library on the subject.

Tolstoy argued with such authority on the scriptural and biblical evidence for Christian nonviolence as to almost single-handedly transform a religious tradition or at least to redirect a significant minority of believers. Since then, many Christians have re-interpreted the social and political implications of their faith. Nonviolence, one might say, is the 19th century counterpart to liberation theology, which has had a similar effect in emphasizing the social implications of Christianity in recent times.

For Americans, Tolstoy's pamphlets have particular significance, since some are based upon his reading of 19th century abolitionists and anarchists whom he admired.

> If I had to address the American people, I would like to thank them for their writers who flourished about the fifties . . . .And I should like to ask the American people why they do not pay more attention to these voices (hardly to be replaced by those of financial and industrial million-aires, or successful generals and admirals), and continue the good work in which they made such hopeful progress.

In a famous polemic, *The Kingdom of God Is Within You* (1894), Tolstoy spoke of the American Quakers who responded to his writings on nonviolence and he quoted extensively from Garrison's "Declaration of Sentiments Adopted by the Peace Convention" (1838) in Boston. Tolstoy also corresponded with Adin Ballou, the founder of the Hopedale Community, and co-founder of the first international peace society in 1854.

At a time when politicians justify an increase in nuclear weapons as a means of encouraging peace negotiations (the infamous "build-down theory" of the Reagan administration, for example), Tolstoy's conclusion to *The Kingdom of God Is Within You* seems especially relevant:

> It has often been said that the invention of the terrible military instruments of murder will put an end to war, and

that war will exhaust itself. This is not true. . . .Let them
be exterminated by thousands and millions, let them be
torn to pieces, men will still continue like stupid cattle to
go to the slaughter, some because they are driven thither
under the lash, others that they may win the decorations
and ribbons which fill their hearts with pride.

In his pamphlets, as in the earlier novels, Tolstoy combined a practical and naturalistic eye for detail with a theoretical
and moral vision. And at the end of his polemics, he returned
to the central question posed by most Russian writers and intellectuals of the 19th century: "What is to be done?" In "Letter to the Liberals" (1896), for example, he answered that
elemental question in this way:

Merely the simple, quiet, truthful carrying on of what you
consider good and needful, quite independently of government and of whether it likes it or not. In other words: standing up for your rights, not as a member of the Literature
Committee, not as a deputy, not as a landowner, not as
a merchant, not even as a member of Parliament; but
standing up for your rights as a rational and free man, and
defending them, not as the rights of local boards or committees are defended, with concessions and compromises,
but without any concessions and compromises, in the only
way in which moral and human dignity can be defended.

Born in Russia, on August 28, 1828 (old-style calendar),
at Yasnaya Polyana, the family estate where he is buried, Leo
Nikolayevich Tolstoy was the fourth son of Count Nikolai Ilyich
Tolstoy. Reared by an aunt after the death of his mother and
father, he studied briefly at Kazan University, and as a young
man spent much of his time gambling and drinking. Later, after
studying law, he established a progressive school for children
of the serfs on his estate. His first stories were published during
his years in the army, at the time of the Crimean war. Leaving
the army in 1856, he traveled about Western Europe, principally
France and Germany. In 1863, the year after his marriage, he
began work on *War and Peace* (1869). Various essays and fiction

followed, including a second major novel, *Anna Karenina* (1878). Although his later fiction is sometimes regarded as inferior to these novels, its popularity steadily increases, particularly *The Death of Ivan Ilyitch* (1886), *The Kreutzer Sonata* (1890), and *Resurrection* (1899).

Internationally famous at fifty, Tolstoy suddenly suffered from bouts of deep despair. In 1879 he wrote,

> My question was the simplest of questions lying in the soul of every man from the foolish child to the wisest elder: It was a question without an answer to which one cannot live, as I had found by experience. It was ''What will come of what I am doing today or shall do tomorrow? What will come of my whole life?''

Re-reading the Old and New Testaments at this time, Tolstoy experienced a conversion to radical Christianity. Subsequently, he wrote extensive commentaries on the Bible, blaming the decline of Christianity, after Constantine, on the church's failure to live up to the religious pacifism of Jesus. Christianity had failed, Tolstoy argued, because it refused to disassociate itself from political power, the sanctification of which he regarded as blasphemous, as the negation of Christianity. ''In truth, the words a 'Christian state' resemble the words 'hot ice.' The thing is either not a State using violence, or it is not Christian,'' he argued.

In 1888, following the birth of her thirteenth and last child, Tolstoy's wife and his chief disciple, Chertkov, quarrelled. From then until the end of his life, the conflicts in the household worsened, as Tolstoy devoted himself to fiction, to Christian anarchism, and to the defense of his followers, the Dukhobers, who were exiled to Canada in 1899. In 1910, in the midst of another crisis at home, Tolstoy left Yasnaya Polyana and, on November 7 of that year, died of pneumonia at Astapovo, at age eighty-two. At his funeral two servants carried a banner at the head of the procession that read, ''Dear Leo Nikolayevich, the memory of your greatness will not die among us, the orphaned peasants of Yasnaya Polyana.''

Tolstoy's writings document the close relationship

between peace and justice issues; and perhaps because he was writing to a most unsympathetic audience, in an era when the very idea of nonviolence was foreign to many Christians, his arguments retain their intensity and vigor a century later. For that reason, almost everyone committed to nonviolence, from Gandhi to the Catholic Worker Movement, from Martin Luther King, Jr., to the youngest draft resister, regards Tolstoy's pamphlets as basic texts.

Of the two great Russian novelists, Tolstoy and Dostoevsky, one usually thinks of Dostoevsky as the more anguished, the person severely tested by the dichotomies of life, and by the evils to which human beings subject one another. But as a prince, as an aristocrat who had much to lose by his conversion, Tolstoy spent much of his later life on a pilgrimage. He died miles from his home, still searching, one might say, for the proper way to live his life as a Christian pacifist.

BY LEO TOLSTOY

The Portable Tolstoy. Edited by John Bayley. New York: Penguin Books, 1978.

Tolstoy's Writings on Civil Disobedience and Non-Violence. New York: Bergman Publishers, 1967.

And many others.

ABOUT LEO TOLSTOY

Simmons, Ernest J. *Introduction to Tolstoy's Writings.* Chicago: University of Chicago Press, 1967.

Steiner, George. *Tolstoy or Dostoevsky: An Essay in the Old Criticism.* New York: Alfred A. Knopf, 1959.

Troyat, Henri. *Tolstoy.* Translated by Nancy Amplioux. Garden City, New York: Doubleday and Co., Inc., 1967.

THOMAS WENTWORTH
HIGGINSON

1823-1911

ANYONE WHO REMEMBERS HIM AT ALL USUALLY THINKS OF
Thomas Wentworth Higginson as the man who spoiled Emily
Dickinson's posthumously published poems. And, in truth, he
did tailor her lines to fit late-19th century fashion. As a consequence, it took sixty years to restore several poems to their
original and superior state.

In literary discussions, in other words, Higginson is pictured as some kind of fool, a judgment based solely upon his conventional taste in poetry. Yet taken at the full, his life is extraordinary, and he had moments of real nobility: courage, certainly, and a strong sense of what was noblest and most democratic in the American experience.

The association between Higginson and Dickinson began on April 16, 1862, when he took from the Worcester, Massachusetts, post office an unsigned letter beginning, "Mr. Higginson — Are you too deeply occupied to say if my verse is alive?" The large envelope contained four poems and, in a smaller envelope, a card with her signature.

Higginson was minister at the time to the Free Church in Worcester, a city midway between the village of Amherst, Dickinson's hometown in western Massachusetts, and Boston. His article in the *Atlantic Monthly,* giving advice to young writers, had prompted Dickinson's letter. Writing many years later, Higginson said: "The impression of a wholly new and original genius was as distinct on my mind at the first reading. . . as it is now." He wrote back immediately with encouragement, and a tense, but cordial friendship blossomed. In one of their exchanges, she later gave her famous definition of poetry: "If I feel physically as if the top of my head were taken off, I know *that* is poetry."

In 1862, Higginson was much the more famous of the two writers and he remained so for another half-century. In the history of nonviolence, however, the years prior to his knowing Dickinson are perhaps the more significant period.

Born in Boston, on December 22, 1823, Thomas Wentworth Higginson was the son of a prosperous merchant and bursar of Harvard College and, through his mother, Louisa Storrow, a descendant of a distinguished colonial family. Visitors to the family home on Boston's Mt. Vernon Street included Adamses, Lowells, and Cabots; and Higginson's own friends later included the most famous literary people of the era: Henry Wadsworth Longfellow, James Russell Lowell, Ralph Waldo Emerson.

In 1837, the year of Emerson's famous Phi Beta Kappa address "The American Scholar," Higginson entered Harvard College. Seven years later, after a brief career as a teacher, he studied at Harvard Divinity School. Lydia Maria Child's *Appeal in Favor of that Class of Americans Called Africans* (1833) had turned his thoughts toward abolitionism by this time, as had the radical theology of Theodore Parker and the eloquent speeches against slavery of Wendell Phillips and William Lloyd Garrison.

During his first assignment as a minister, in Newburyport, Massachusetts, Higginson committed himself to a number of social reforms, including the abolition of slavery and of capital punishment. He led a campaign to establish a free evening school for illiterate adults and joined John Greenleaf Whittier in supporting workers in nearby Salisbury who advocated the ten-hour day (when fourteen hours was common).

Higginson's characteristic response to the Fugitive Slave Law of 1850 was immediate and firm: "Is it not a crime to permit a fellow being carried into slavery? . . . We should in all cases disobey the law and show our good citizenship by taking the penalty." In 1852, after accepting a call to the Free Church of Worcester, he campaigned in that "new cradle of liberty" for temperance, women's rights, penal and land reform, as well as for abolitionism and the ten-hour day. The following year he shared the platform at the Massachusetts Anti-Slavery Society in Boston with Garrison, Abby and Stephen Foster, and Lucy Stone. Shortly afterward, in New York, he led a boycott of a national meeting of the World Temperance Committee that threatened to exclude women, and joined Foster, Stone, Susan B. Anthony, Lucretia Mott, and Elizabeth Cady Stanton in a public protest.

In May 1854, Higginson led an abortive attempt to rescue a fugitive slave from the Court House in Boston; returning to Worcester that evening, his chin bandaged as a result of a wound suffered in the struggle, he addressed a thousand people. Later that fall he helped prevent the arrest of another slave, saying: "I am not responsible for the evils of the whole world, but I am responsible for what happens beside my own doorstep."

The crusade against slavery took Higginson to the Midwest, particularly Kansas, where many abolitionists settled in order to make sure that the state entered the union on the side of freedom. He wrote,

> Under the influence of Slavery, we are rapidly relapsing
> into that state of barbarism in which every man must rely
> on his own right hand for his protection. . . .For myself
> existence looks worthless under such circumstances. I
> respect law and order, but as the ancient Persian sage said,
> "*Always* to obey the law, virtue must relax much of her
> vigor." I see, now, that while Slavery is national, law and
> order must constantly be on the wrong side.

In the 1860s, Thomas Wentworth Higginson devoted
himself more directly to violent means of solving the conflict,
including support for John Brown. His *Black Rebellion: A Selection from Travellers and Outlaws,* based upon official reports, diaries,
memoirs, and newspapers, contains five black slave narratives.
During the Civil War, Higginson became the commander of
the first black regiment.

In the years following the Civil War and the death of his
wife, Higginson devoted himself to literature, to biographies of
Emerson, Margaret Fuller, and to literary history, including
essays on "the belle of Amherst" when her poems were first
published.

Today Dickinson's and Higginson's fortunes are almost
totally reversed. She is recognized throughout the world as one
of the two great American poets of the 19th century, while he
is practically unknown, in spite of his many contributions to social
reform as a militant abolitionist and feminist.

Unlike many of his Brahmin contemporaries, Higgin-
son took considerable risks during his lifetime to correct the injustices of his time and to uphold the values which he regarded
as essential to a just social order. With Garrison, the Fosters,
and Lucy Stone, at whose marriage Higginson officiated, he is
an important figure in the American tradition of nonviolence.
Even with his inconsistencies and his limited skills as a critic,
he helped to reconcile the conflict between the promise of
American life and its unjust treatment of blacks, working people,
and women.

BY THOMAS WENTWORTH HIGGINSON

"Massachusetts in Mourning." *Civil Disobedience in America: A Documentary History.* Edited by David R. Weber. Ithaca, N.Y.; Cornell University Press, 1978.

Black Rebellion: A Selection From Travellers and Outlaws. New York: Arno Press and the New York Times, 1969.

And many others.

ABOUT THOMAS WENTWORTH HIGGINSON

Edelstein, Tilder G. *Strange Enthusiasm: A Life of Thomas Wentworth Higginson.* New Haven: Yale University Press, 1968.

Meyer, Harold N. *Colonel of the Black Regiment: The Life of Thomas Wentworth Higginson.* New York: W.W. Norton Co., 1967.

Bibliography of American Literature. Edited by Jacob Blanck, vol. 4, New Haven, Connecticut: Yale University Press, 1963.

LUCY STONE

1818-1893

ALTHOUGH SHE WAS DRAWN TO POLITICAL ACTIVISM THROUGH the abolitionist movement, her first and major concern was woman's rights. From the time she was very young, Lucy Stone resented the limitations imposed upon women, as well as the low pay they received as teachers. Her associations, nonetheless, among abolitionists—Abigail and Stephen Foster, Thomas

Wentworth Higginson, William Lloyd Garrison, and Julia Ward Howe—strengthened and heightened her social awareness. So did her husband's family, whose members included the first woman to be awarded a medical degree in this country and the first to be ordained a minister.

Born in West Brookfield, Massachusetts, on August 13, 1818, Lucy Stone identified, even as a young child, with the hard lot of her mother. She resented the fact that the Congregational Church allowed her no vote, and as she listened to a pastoral letter censuring women for speaking in public, she turned to a cousin next to her and said, "If I ever had anything to say in public, I should say it, and all the more because of the Pastoral Letter."

Against the advice of her father, Stone resolved to study Greek and Hebrew in an effort to correct the "inaccuracies" of the Bible that justified the subjugation of women. After brief periods at two women's seminaries near her home, she traveled to Ohio to study at Oberlin College, known as a center for abolitionism. There she arranged for her friends Abigail and Stephen Foster to speak, but moved the event to a nearby church when the college barred them from the campus. An honor graduate, Stone refused to give a commencement address, since women were not allowed to speak to "promiscuous" audiences, that is, mixed groups of men and women. After her graduation, the Fosters and Garrison encouraged Stone in her agitation against slavery, but she eventually declared her primary vocation: "I was a woman before I was an abolitionist. I must speak for the women."

Determined to remain single, Stone was nonetheless courted by Henry Browne Blackwell, a Cincinnati businessman from a family of reformers. They married in 1855 in a ceremony protesting laws that were oppressive to women. She retained her own name, rather than follow the usual custom of taking her husband's. They had one child, a daughter, who later joined her mother and father as an editor of *Woman's Journal.*

Although Stone had won Susan B. Anthony to the feminist cause, the two later quarrelled over ways to win equal rights for women. Stone regarded Anthony and Elizabeth Cady Stanton as rather reckless, particularly after they accepted help from a man known for his attacks on black people. Over the years, enmity increased between the two wings of the feminist movement. When Julia Ward Howe brought the news, to an ailing Lucy Stone, that Mrs. Stanton was dying, "Lucy speculated that the cause of death would probably be apoplexy, and remarked how odd it would be if the first person she met on the other side was Mrs. Stanton," according to Leslie Wheeler. Stone died in her home in Dorchester, Massachusetts, in 1893, not long after returning from the Columbian Exposition in Chicago, where she delivered her last lecture.

Stone's correspondence with her husband, seven years her junior, is surprisingly modern in recording their efforts to maintain a loving, but independent relationship. "How soon the character of the race would change," she wrote to him in 1853, "if pure, and equal, real marriages would take the place of the horrible relations that now bear that sacred name." As with Abigail Foster, she worked hard to combine marriage, motherhood, and a vital career, and thus to establish a precedent for future generations of women.

A source of strength for Stone and Blackwell was the community of people around them. Continual resistance to the status quo is seldom possible without a support system, and the lives of many of the famous literary and political figures of the mid-19th century suggest the power of cooperation and mutual aid, even among people whose personalities conflict. This is observable among feminists and abolitionists, as well as among artists of the American Renaissance, Emerson and Thoreau, Hawthorne and the Brook Farm community.

Known as an effective speaker and admired by her many associates, Stone had a reputation for standing her ground, even against formidable opposition such as Elizabeth Cady Stanton. Scholars and historians continue to debate the effectiveness of each of the two women's approaches to social change. But in a letter on tactics, written to Stanton on October 19, 1869, Stone indicated her clear-headedness about her goals and the politics of achieving them. She explained the wisdom of having two feminist societies, each having the benefit of national names, each attracting those who naturally belong to it [in order to] secure the active cooperation of *all* friends of the cause, better than either could do alone. People will differ as to what they consider the best methods and means. The true wisdom is not to ignore, but to provide for the fact.

So far as she had influence, Stone said, her society would

never be an enemy or antagonist of yours in any way. It will simply fill a field and combine forces, which yours does not. I shall rejoice when any of the onerous (sic) works are carried, no matter who does it.

In a final remark to her sister-in-conflict, Stone expressed the hope that sustained her through many exhausting campaigns for women's rights: "Your little girls and mine will reap the easy harvest which it costs so much to sow."

According to tradition, Lucy Stone was herself the first woman to speak from a pulpit in Massachusetts or to receive a B.A. degree (Oberlin College, 1847). "An innovator to the end," as Louis Filler has said, "she was the first person also to be cremated in New England." Tireless, persistent, and occasionally misunderstood, she was an editor and lecturer for over forty years.

BY LUCY STONE

Loving Warriors: Selected Letters of Lucy Stone and Henry B. Blackwell. Edited by Leslie Wheeler. New York: The Dial Press, 1981.

ABOUT LUCY STONE

Blackwell, Alice Stone. *Lucy Stone.* New York: Kraus Reprint Co., 1930, 1971.

Filler, Louis. "Stone." In *Notable American Women, 1607-1950: A Biographical Dictionary,* vol. III. Edited by Edward T. James and Janet W. James. Cambridge, Mass.: Harvard University Press, 1971, 387-90.

Hays, Elinor Rice. *Morning Star: A Biography of Lucy Stone, 1818-1893.* New York: Harcourt, Brace and World, 1961.

ABIGAIL KELLEY

1811-1887

AND

STEPHEN SYMONDS FOSTER

1809-1881

THE DISAPPEARANCE OF SIGNIFICANT FIGURES FROM AMERICAN history robs successive generations of models for moral and political responsibility. As a consequence married couples, among others who try to center their lives on justice issues, are seldom presented with flesh-and-blood examples of how to live their lives.

In some instances, men and women sacrifice their spouses

in order to follow vocations for social justice. In others, one of them lives in the background, maintaining the family and caring for the children, while the other pursues a public life. In a few instances, however, husbands and wives successfully maintain two vocations, the one to the social order and the one to one another. This was particularly true of Abigail Kelley and Stephen Symonds Foster, both of whom appear in the *Dictionary of American Biography*, though Abby is generally regarded as the more famous of the two.

Both people, however, deserve a special place in the history of nonviolence, she as an abolitionist, feminist, and tax resister, he as a faithful apostle of nonviolence, abolitionist, and war resister. Their correspondence both before their marriage and during the years each stayed at home, while the other took to the circuit on behalf of abolitionism, is a remarkable record of a union that was oppressive to neither, that was liberating for both. That respect and love are reflected in a tribute Stephen wrote for Abby late in their lives: "O, how I wish she could be *young* again, to thrill the very air with her fiery denunciations. . . . Her work, I fear, is nearly done on earth, but she has large investments in Heaven. In moral power I have never known her equal, and never shall."

Each of them came to marriage in 1845 with a dedication to social justice and something of a career based upon these concerns. Abby had advocated immediate abolition of slavery since the early 1830s, when she first heard William Lloyd Garrison speak, and Stephen had taken various risks in resisting slavery and militarism since his undergraduate days at Dartmouth College.

Born in Pelham, Massachusetts, on January 15, 1811, Abigail Kelley was the daughter of Irish Quakers. She attended schools in Worcester, Massachusetts, where her parents, prosperous farmers, moved soon after Abby was born, as well as the Friends School in Providence, Rhode Island. At the time she heard Garrison, she was teaching in Lynn, Massachusetts, and later headed a five-woman delegation to the National Female Anti-Slavery Society convention in New York. In 1839, she left teaching altogether in order to devote full-time to abolitionism, confessing to Theodore Weld at the time that she had "nothing to start upon, nothing to commend me to the notice or favor of any, no name, no reputation, no scrip, neither money in my purse.''

Abby Kelley proved, nonetheless, to be an effective champion of the cause, traveling throughout New England, New York, and into the Midwest, speaking to large and appreciative audiences, and co-editing the *Anti-Slavery Bugle*. Frequently she was ridiculed for speaking to ''promiscuous'' audiences (that is, audiences of men and women), and for traveling about with men, both black and white. But she remained faithful to her motto: ''Go where you are least wanted, for there you are most needed.''

The very qualities that scandalized conventional souls were the ones that attracted Stephen Foster. As a vigorous and independent agitator for justice, he had long faced the kind of opposition that he occasionally provoked. Born in southern New Hampshire, on November 17, 1809, the ninth of twelve children, Stephen Symonds Foster graduated from Dartmouth College in 1838 and went to study for a time at Union Theological Seminary in New York. He had been jailed in Hanover, New Hampshire, for refusing to perform military duty at college, and left Union when the administration refused permission for a room to hold an antiwar meeting. Later, as an itinerant preacher, he traveled New England, asking to speak to congregations, particularly if they had not endorsed abolitionism, and in 1843 he published a popular pamphlet entitled *The Brotherhood of Thieves; or, A True Picture of the American Church and Clergy*. It argued that any church that refused to condemn slavery was ''more corrupt and profligate than any house of ill fame in the city of New York. . . .''

The 1850s were particularly hectic years for the Fosters, with Stephen and then Abby on speaking tours, while the other cared for their daughter, ''Alla,'' born in 1847. That decade saw the first National Woman's Rights Conventions at Seneca Falls, New York, in 1848, and in Worcester, in 1850 and 1851, in which Abigail had an active part. During these years, particularly because of the Fugitive Slave Law of 1850, the Foster home in Worcester was a busy station on the underground railway. In 1854 an incident involving a federal marshall, who came to arrest a former slave, and the Worcester Vigilance

Committee, which resisted him, tested Stephen's dedication to nonviolence. With two others, Foster escorted the arresting officer through a hostile crowd of abolitionists and onto a train back to Boston, to protect him from harm. In a letter to Abigail, Stephen described the conflict within himself; as an abolitionist, he opposed everything the officer stood for, but as a pacifist, he could not allow anyone to assault him.

> I have often been myself the object of popular rage, as you well know, but never did I feel half the anxiety for my own life which I felt for his, or make half the effort to save it. There, I felt that the honor of our cause was at stake, and for the moment, my heart yearned almost with agony for a *bloodless* victory.

The Fosters were also tax resisters, maintaining that they owed no allegiance to a government which allowed Abigail no vote and little voice in its proceedings. Only in old age, when Stephen was ill and Abigail was exhausted from a lifetime of agitation, did they finally pay the taxes to regain a title to their land. Stephen died in 1881 and Abigail in 1887, in Worcester; their home, near Tatnuck Square, is preserved and named on the National Register.

Wendell Phillips said of Stephen, who was noted for his resonant voice and his colorful denunciations of slaveholders, ''It needed something to shake New England and stun it into listening. He was the man, and offered himself for the martyrdom.'' A writer for the *Woman's Journal* wrote, at the time of Abigail's death:

> The women of this land owe this woman more than to any other human being, a debt of gratitude for the doors she opened for them to enter, for the paths she made smooth for them with her own bleeding feet, for the courage and conscientiousness and the faithfulness with which, amid persecution and reviling, she made the way clear for them to walk safely.

And best of all, their union was a happy one, both for the couple and for abolitionism, as Abigail wrote to a female friend:

I wish to congratulate the cause on the fact that since our marriage, meetings have been much more successful than heretofore. We realize that even in the anti-slavery cause a whole man and a whole woman are far better than a half-man and a half-woman.

BY STEPHEN SYMONDS FOSTER

The Brotherhood of Thieves, or a True Picture of the American Church and Clergy. New York: Arno Press, 1863, 1866 (1969).

ABOUT ABIGAIL KELLEY
AND
STEPHEN SYMONDS FOSTER

Bacon, Margaret Hope. *I Speak for My Slave Sister: The Life of Abby Kelley Foster.* New York: Thomas Y. Crowell, 1974.

Burkett, Nancy. *Abby Kelley Foster and Stephen S. Foster.* Worcester, Mass.: Worcester Bicentennial Commission, 1976.

Melder, Keith E. "Abigail Kelley Foster." In *Notable American Women, 1607-1950: A Biographical Dictionary,* vol. I. Edited by Edward T. James and Janet W. James. Cambridge, Mass.: Harvard University Press, 1971.

JOHN HENRY NEWMAN

1801-1890

THE MAN FOR WHOM NEWMAN CENTERS ARE NAMED, ON COLLEGE and university campuses across the United States, is not as well known or as widely read as he once was. His books, formerly required reading in Catholic schools and colleges, are seldom mentioned. His influence, in fact, appears to be more evident at large state universities than in church-related colleges.

Whatever the cause for this change, it is proper still to ask why anyone concerned about social justice should remember this scholarly Victorian gentleman. And young people who have never heard of John Henry Newman are quite right in expecting older readers to justify their admiration for him. In doing so, I shall emphasize the man rather than his writings, his life rather than his thought.

Regarded as the spiritual father of the Second Vatican Council, he is the subject of numerous books, including several rather dense and even obtuse philosophical treatises. Sometimes such discussions veil the man, at a time when his personal example, rather than his scholarship, may rightfully be regarded as our principal concern. At present, one needs to speak as directly about Newman as he spoke about public matters in his sermons, in letters to the London *Times,* and in defense of his religious opinions, *Apologia Pro Vita Sua* (1864). "A life—how different from one's own," George Eliot, Newman's contemporary, said of the latter book, "yet with how close a fellowship in its needs and burdens."

A century later Newman's life appears, on the surface, as a series of triumphs. Born in 1801, in London, the oldest child of a successful banker and the descendent of a French Hugenot family, Newman excelled as a young student before entering Trinity College, Oxford, at the age of 16. In spite of a disappointing finish as an undergraduate, he was elected a fellow of Oriel College at 22, and after his ordination as an Anglican clergyman, became Vicar of the University Church of St. Mary the Virgin in 1828. Shortly afterward, the Oxford Movement and the widely circulated *Tracts for the Times* made him an international figure. Popular as a tutor at Oxford University and as a preacher, as well as a faithful pastor of a country parish, he was loved and admired especially among the laity.

Received into the Roman Catholic Church in 1845, Newman became a priest of the Oratory of St. Philip Neri in Rome shortly afterward. Appointed Rector of the Catholic University in Ireland in 1854, which led eventually to the present University College, Newman gave a series of lectures on the nature of "liberal education," eventually published as *The Idea of a University.* In a famous autobiography, he successfully defended himself when his integrity as a man and thinker was questioned. Elected the first honorary fellow of his old college at Oxford, he was nominated to the College of Cardinals in 1879 by the new pope, Leo XIII. Through special permission, he remained at Birmingham Oratory, his home until his death, at 89, on August 11, 1890.

The successes of Newman's life are well-known and easily described, but the frustrations, the disappointments, and the many defeats—so often the source of his vigorous, argumentative essays and lyric poems—are less fully appreciated. His most famous poem, "Lead, Kindly Light," written in dejection near Sicily, records one of several such personal crises.

A man of exceptional gifts—poet, musician, theologian, historian, minister—he was uncertain, like many Victorians, about how best to use those gifts. A leader of the Oxford Movement, which had political and moral implications for the Church of England, as well as for the university, he stunned his powerful and wealthy friends by following what was for him the logical path to Rome. Once there, he found himself mistrusted and spied upon, regarded with alarm and even with envy, leading to this comment in his journal in 1861: "Since I have been a Catholic, I seem to myself to have had nothing but failure personally."

Of the many frustrations Newman endured, several stand out. Appointed Rector of the Catholic University in Ireland, he found after four years that support from the Irish hierarchy and even from the laity had disappeared. His appointment as a bishop was mysteriously dropped when a suspicious Irish prelate intervened. Asked to undertake a new translation of the Bible, he discovered, on accepting the task, that requests for contributions were met with total silence.

A persistent pattern emerged of Newman's being recommended for a position that his intelligence and leadership had prepared him for, only to have the case undermined by a higher ecclesiastical authority. This happened so many times that one begins to understand why the Red Hat meant so much to him. "Now the Pope in his generosity has taken this reproach simply away," Newman wrote to a friend after his election to the College of Cardinals, "and it is wonderful Providence, that even before my death acquital of me comes, which I knew would come some day or another, though not in my lifetime.''

One would hardly guess from the public record that Newman felt anything but affirmation and confidence over the years, about his many projects: the founding of a school for boys and ministry to the working people of Birmingham, in a parish where he sometimes doubled as organist and violinist; advice for a succession of students and adults, including Gerard Manley Hopkins, who followed him into the Catholic Church; and the torrent of letters to newspapers on major public issues of the day; sermons, lectures, novels, poetry, biographies of the saints (more than thirty published volumes in all, with perhaps twice again as many volumes in personal correspondence, notebooks, and diaries). Following Newman's activities, one is reminded of E.P. Thompson's comment about William Morris, another Victorian artist and pamphleteer, that it is impossible to understand how one man did so much during certain periods of his life.

As a teacher, I am challenged more by Newman's style than by the ''rightness'' of his philosophy of education or religion. By ''style'' I mean, as he said, ''a living into thought.'' Throughout his life as a writer and thinker, he upheld a humanitarian vision of education when the utilitarians tried to make the university less personal and moral than it should be. At the same time, he upheld an expansive vision of the church, when the ultramontanes (the reactionary and overly defensive Romanists) wanted to make it less catholic and intellectual than it need be. He remained faithful to that vision when people around him wanted to make both institutions narrow and apologetic.

And Newman never regarded religion as a censor of the university, as it has sometimes been used by Catholic higher education. Theology, he thought, must be subjected to the same honest inquiry as every other science, even if that investigation brought it into public controversy. ''The energy of the human intellect 'does from opposition grow,' '' he said in the *Apologia*.

Having Newman nearby, as his religious superiors learned, was rather like having a time-bomb in your midst. He was a man who followed his vocation, rather than one who merely did the expected thing. When he became a Catholic, many assumed that he would live in sophisticated London, preparing converts for the church. He preferred to work in industrial

Birmingham, preparing the church for converts. His ministry was to the poor and to immigrants, clergy and laity who benefitted from his learning and talent.

Intellectual inquiry was as central to Newman's attitude toward education and the common good, one might say, as conscience was to his attitude toward religious belief. Newman's life and writings cast an informing light on public affairs, and for that reason a Newman revival (a re-reading and reconsideration of his life) is appropriate to a later century, as full of doubt, uncertainty, and confusion as his own.

Or, to put it another way, paraphrasing Wordsworth's sonnet to Milton, "Newman, we have need of you at this hour." We need his deep learning and patient skill as a teacher, his energy and humility, his love of music and poetry, his pastoral care, and especially his steadfastness in the face of intellectual indifference, inside and outside the university and the church.

BY JOHN HENRY NEWMAN

The Idea of a University. Edited by Martin J. Svaglic. University of Notre Dame Press, 1982.

Apologia Pro Vita Sua. Edited by David DeLaura. New York: W.W. Norton, 1968.

The Essential Newman. Edited by Vincent Ferrer Blehl. New York: New American Library, 1963.

And many others.

ABOUT JOHN HENRY NEWMAN

Martin, Brian. *John Henry Newman: His Life and Work.* New York: Oxford University Press, 1982.

Trevor, Meriol. *Newman's Journey*. Cleveland: Collins and World, 1977.

_____.*Newman Pillar of the Cloud*. London: Macmillan and Company, 1962.

_____.*Newman Light in Winter*. London: Macmillan and Company, 1962.

THOMAS PAINE

1737-1809

AMONG THOSE WHO SPENT THEIR LIVES ADVOCATING PEACE WITH
justice, few names are nobler than that of Thomas Paine. English
by birth, but American by choice and temperament, he called
himself a citizen of the world. His motto: ''My country is the
world; to do good is my religion.'' To a remarkable degree
Paine's life and writing are one, and his biography follows

naturally from the concerns of his libertarian pamphlets.

As a literary radical, Paine brought his background as a working class citizen to everything he wrote, from his first pamphlet advocating higher wages for overworked and underpaid civil employees, to *Common Sense, Rights of Man,* and *Agrarian Justice.* Throughout he exhibited a genius for making complex ideas, economic and political truths, understandable to a large audience, and his writings were among the first bestsellers. The list of humanitarian causes aided by his pamphlets reads like a list of democratic movements of the past three centuries: abolitionism, land reform, women's rights, better conditions for workers, resistance to imperialism, civil rights. Although occasionally impudent and impetuous in his personal behavior, he remained faithful to the common people to the end of his life, championing their cause and working in their interest. Many poor people benefited from his generosity and not a few tyrants suffered because of his forthrightness in the cause of liberty.

Thomas Paine (spelled originally without the ''e'') was born in Thetford, seventy miles northeast of London, on January 29, 1737. His mother, an Anglican, was the daughter of an attorney; his father, a Quaker, was a small farmer and staymaker. In Paine's life and writings, his Quaker association remained significant, as the French radical, Marat, spitefully pointed out years later. When Paine voted against the execution of Louis XVI, in the French assembly, Marat claimed Paine did so because Quakers opposed capital punishment. For practical reasons, many Frenchmen regretted afterward their failure to follow Paine's advice.

After several years of schooling, the young Paine worked as an apprentice in his father's shop, went to sea, married, and became an excise officer in the town of Lewes. Widowed by one woman, he married again, only to be legally separated shortly afterward.

In 1774, Paine's friend, Benjamin Franklin, provided references for the younger man's move to the American colonies. A little over a year later, in Philadelphia, he published *Common Sense,* which helped to unite the colonies against a common foe, and to fan the fires of revolution in America and then abroad.

Two years later, his *Crisis* papers championed the

American cause against Great Britain and won support among the merchant class for the Revolution. George Washington and others praised Paine's papers as central to the American victory, and although congress eventually voted Paine a stipend for his writing, a statement in *American Crisis II* accurately described his usual generosity:

> My writing I have always given away, reserving only the expense of printing and paper, and sometimes not even that. I never courted fame or interest, and my manner of life, to those who know it, will justify what I say. My study is to be useful.

Paine subsequently alienated many powerful politicians by exposing lies and deceit in the new government; and in later years, only Thomas Jefferson remained loyal to him. As with his later attacks on superstition and traditional religion, his exposes of political skulduggery prejudiced early commentators, especially the Federalists, against him.

Away from America between 1787 and 1802, Paine played a significant role in the French Revolution, and nearly lost his life for opposing the extreme policies of Robespierre. In prison outside Paris, he continued writing essays and poems, read and revised *The Age of Reason.* Earlier, *Rights of Man* (1791), an attack on Edmund Burke and a defense of the *French Declaration of the Rights of Man and the Citizen,* led to charges of sedition in his native England, from which he was banished, narrowly escaping imprisonment in 1792.

The Age of Reason: Being an Investigation of True and of Fabulous Theology (1794-96) attempted to purge institutional religion of its abuses, "lest in the general wreck of superstition, of false systems of government, and false theology, we lose sight of morality, of humanity, and of theology that is true." The book caused a furor in Europe, as well as in the United States, after Paine's return in 1802. He died seven years later, on June 8, 1809, in Greenwich Village, New York City.

A scurrilous biography shortly after Paine's death provoked controversy over his life and writings once again, and later critics, such as Theodore Roosevelt, mistakenly regarded Paine as an atheist. Yet against all detractors, Paine's own defense, in response to a royal proclamation suppressing *Rights of Man*, accurately described his central concerns:

> If, to expose the fraud and imposition of monarchy, and every species of hereditary government—to less the oppression of taxes—to propose plans for the education of helpless infancy, and the comfortable support of the aged and distressed—to endeavor to conciliate nations to each other—to extirpate the horrid practice of war—to promote universal peace, and civilization, and the commerce—and to break the chains of political superstititon, and raise degraded man to his proper rank—if these things be libellous, let me live the life of a Libeller, and let the name of LIBELLER be engraved on my tomb.

For subsequent libertarians, William Lloyd Garrison and Walt Whitman, Eugene Victor Debs and Randolph Bourne, Paine was an inspiration and a guide, and his writing espouses values and programs still associated with nonviolent social change.

Like many American radicals, Paine hated privilege and pretention, and reacted strongly against anything that smacked of condescension toward the down-and-out, among whom he spent his earliest years. He was, to the end of his days, the supreme democrat, and his eloquent indictment of poverty, from *Agrarian Justice,* speaks to the economic injustice of the present world, as it did two centuries ago:

> The rugged face of society, checkered with the extremes of affluence and want, proves that some extraordinary violence has been committed upon it, and calls on justice for redress. The great mass of the poor in all countries are become an hereditary race, and it is next to impossible for them to get out of that state of themselves. . . . It is not charity but a right, not bounty but justice, that I am pleading for. The present state of civilization is as odious as it is unjust. . . . The contrast of affluence and wretchedness continually meeting and offending the eye is like dead and living bodies chained together.

BY THOMAS PAINE

The Complete Writings of Thomas Paine, 2 vols. Edited by Philip Foner. New York: The Citadel Press, 1945.

Thomas Paine: Representative Selections, with Introduction, Bibliography, and Notes. Revised. Edited by Harry Hayden Clark. New York: Hill and Wang, 1961.

ABOUT THOMAS PAINE

Aldridge, Alfred Owen. *Man of Reason: The Life of Thomas Paine.* Philadelphia: J.B. Lippincott Co., 1959.

Fennessy, R.R. *Burke, Paine, and the Rights of Man: A Difference of Political Opinions.* The Hague, 1963.

Foner, Eric. *Tom Paine and Revolutionary America.* New York: Oxford University Press, 1976.

Hawke, David Freeman. *Paine.* New York: Harper and Row, 1974.

True, Michael. "Thomas Paine." In *American Writers,* supplement I, part 2. Edited by Leonard Unger. New York: Charles Scribners Sons, 1979, 501-25.